Other Books by and about Karel Čapek
from Catbird Press

Toward the Radical Center: A Karel Čapek Reader
edited by Peter Kussi, foreword by Arthur Miller

War with the Newts translated by Ewald Osers

Cross Roads translated by Norma Comrada

Karel Čapek – Life and Work by Ivan Klíma
translated by Norma Comrada

Three Novels translated by M. & R. Weatherall

Apocryphal Tales translated by Norma Comrada

Tales from Two Pockets translated by Norma Comrada

TALKS WITH
T. G. MASARYK

by Karel Čapek

Translated from the Czech
by Michael Henry Heim

CATBIRD PRESS
A Garrigue Book

CATBIRD PRESS
16 Windsor Road, North Haven, CT 06473
www.catbirdpress.com
203-230-2391; info@catbirdpress.com

Our books are distributed by Independent Publishers Group

Sony ISBN 978-1-936053-06-3
Kindle ISBN 978-1-936053-07-0
Adobe ISBN 978-1-936053-08-7

Library of Congress Cataloging-in-Publication Data

Masaryk, T. G.. (Tomáš Garrigue), 1850-1937.
[Hovory s T.G. Masarykem. English. Selections]
Talks with T. G. Masaryk / by Karel Čapek ; translated from the Czech by Dora Round ;
edited by Michael Henry Heim.
Consists of parts I, II, and IV of the four-part biography, "Hovory s T. G. Masarykem."
Parts I and II were published as "President Masaryk tells his story," by G. P. Putnam's Sons
in 1935; Part III was published as "Masaryk on thought and life," by Allen & Unwin in
1938. Includes bibliographical references.
ISBN 0-945774-26-5 : $13.95
1. Masaryk, T. G. (Tomáš Garrigue), 1850-1937--Interviews.
2. Presidents--Czechoslovakia--Interviews. I. Čapek, Karel,
1890-1938. II. Round, Dora. III. Heim, Michael Henry.
IV. Masaryk, T. G.. (Tomáš Garrigue), 1850-1937. President Masaryk tells his story. V.
Masaryk, T. G. (Tomáš Garrigue), 1850-1937. Masaryk on thought and life. VI. Title.
DB2191.M38A513 1995
943.7'032'092--dc20
94-42805 CIP

CONTENTS

Translator's Foreword

Talks with T. G. Masaryk, a collaborative effort between the first president of the First Czechoslovak Republic, Tomáš Garrigue Masaryk, and the novelist, playwright, and journalist Karel Čapek originally appeared in three parts: *Youth* (1928) and *Life and Work* (1931), which take the form of an autobiographical monologue; and *Thought and Life* (1935), a philosophical dialogue. The first and second parts were published in a somewhat abridged English translation by Dora Round as *President Masaryk Tells His Story* (1934 in the United Kingdom, 1935 in the United States); the third part in an English translation by M. & R. Weatherall as *Masaryk on Thought on Life* (1938 in the United Kingdom, 1971 in the United States). The current volume includes the complete texts of parts one and two, as well as "Silence with T. G. Masaryk," an essay by Čapek about the talks themselves, published in 1935. "Silence" did not appear in either of the English-language volumes. Moreover, this is a substantially new translation of the first and second parts.

Talks with T. G. Masaryk might be called a "third-person autobiography." Masaryk was extremely popular as President, but he eventually found himself turning into a figurehead. By teaming up with Čapek, the nation's unofficial poet laureate, he was able to convey his position on a number of moral and political issues. His thoughts deserve to be better known in and of themselves, and also because they have gained new relevance in the post-Communist context.

Masaryk makes frequent reference to figures and events unfamiliar to non-Czech readers. I have provided notes only for those most relevant to the text, marking them with an asterisk the first time they occur. The notes can be found at the back of the volume.

—Michael Henry Heim

Publisher's Foreword

T. G. Masaryk had a great deal of luck when he was alive, but little since he died in 1937. A year after his death, Hitler invaded Czechoslovakia and Masaryk became a democratic patriot not to be spoken of. Three years after the Germans were defeated, the Communists staged a coup and Masaryk became a bourgeois capitalist not to be spoken of. To add insult to injury, in 1969 Claire Sterling wrote a book "proving" that Masaryk's son Jan, the Foreign Secretary, had been pushed out a window by the Communists as part of their 1948 coup. This cold-war book became a bestseller and eclipsed the memory of Jan's far greater father, especially in the United States.

Thus even though Masaryk revered America and what it stands for, married an American, sent his children to live and work in America, and created the only Central European state based on American democratic principles and the only one able to withstand fascist tendencies throughout the 1930s, his life and ideas are known to only a tiny number of Americans, and to almost none under sixty. We have let Lenin, Hitler, and Stalin win the battle for our attention against a man whom they saw as a great Central European antagonist. I hope this edition will at least partly counterbalance this crime.

Talks with T. G. Masaryk is a remarkable work of biography. First of all, it brings together not only one nation's greatest writer and greatest political leader, but two of the greatest writers and political figures of the last century. That alone is worth the price of admission.

But in addition, this book takes a rare form. It is closest to what is now known as "oral biography," which involves recording and then transcribing a person's memories. However, Čapek did not have a tape recorder; he did not even take notes during much of the talks. Thus, the result is not a transcription, but rather an independent work composed by Čapek in the voice of Masaryk. It is a literary creation in the form of an autobiography, but based on actual talks that occurred over a number of years. Moreover, nowhere do Čapek's questions and comments appear in the book, an amazing feat of humility. There may be another such book somewhere in world literature, but I have not yet heard of it.

Also notable about this book is the fact that a president, not to mention one in his 70s, could be so open about himself, about his personal life, his failings, his psychological and ethical conflicts. There are definitely signs of myth-making in this book, but it is an exceptionally honest self-portrayal of a major political figure. Its reappearance is especially timely for a generation familiar with former Czech President Václav Havel, whose ideas arise out of Masaryk's in many ways.

More than any other book, this is the one that sparked my fascination with Czech culture and history. It was the first of Čapek's books I read, and it introduced me to a man who intrigued me so much that I taught myself Czech in order to make a stab at a biography of him. I soon found that learning Czech, as hard as it was, was a thousand times easier than taking on Tomáš Garrigue Masaryk.

Why was I so taken with him? Not just because he is the closest thing to a Philosopher-King I had come across (he actually was a philosophy professor before going into politics). I was more struck by the man himself, a bundle of conflicts who formed a harmonious whole, and a great one. I found Masaryk in many ways unattractive — didactic, self-righteous, self-aggrandizing, obsessed with his own death — yet I found his wisdom, his courage, his radical centrism, his integrity, and his humanity so attractive, I came to see his failings as part and parcel of his greatness.

If you have ever wondered why Catbird's Czech literature is published under the Garrigue Books imprint, it will now become more clear. Not only is Garrigue the G. in T. G. Masaryk, it is also the maiden name of his wife, Charlotte Garrigue Masaryk, in whose honor the imprint was named. Charlotte Garrigue was the American most involved in the culture and history of Czechoslovakia, as its first first lady, and long before that as well. Masaryk, a women's libber for the time, took his wife's maiden name at the time of their marriage.

I am proud to be able to publish this singular book in a new translation, and in the first complete, correct, and paperback edition available in English.

—Robert Wechsler

Chronology of Masaryk's Life

1850 - Born on 7 March in Hodonín, Moravia, Austria. Lived in various villages in the area, especially Čejkovice.

1862 - Entered secondary school in Hustopeč, Moravia.

1864 - Apprenticed to a locksmith in Vienna, then to a blacksmith in Čejč, Moravia. Served as assistant teacher at the local elementary school.

1865 - Entered Gymnasium in Brno, the largest city in Moravia.

1869 - Entered Academic Gymnasium in Vienna.

1872 - Entered University of Vienna.

1876 - Received doctorate in philosopohy and went to the University of Leipzig in the autumn.

1877 - Met Charlotte Garrigue, an American studying music in Leipzig.

1878 - Went to the United States to marry Charlotte Garrigue. Returned to Vienna and lectured at the University, tutored, and reworked his thesis on suicide.

1882 - Went to teach at the new Czech University in Prague.

1884 - Founded a journal called the *Athenaeum*.

1886 - Manuscripts Controversy.

1887 - First stay in Russia.

1889 - Co-founded Realist faction within Young Czech Party.

1890 - Karel Čapek born on 9 January in Northern Bohemia.

1891 - First elected to Parliament. Represented the Young Czech Party.

1893 - Founded a journal called *Naše doba* (Our Times).

1899 - Hilsner affair.

1902 - Second trip to the United States. Lectured in Chicago.

1907 - Third trip to the United States. Lectured in various cities.

1909 - Attended the Zagreb and Friedjung trials.

1914 - Abroad at the outbreak of the World War. Went to Prague, then Rome in the interest of the Czech cause.

1915 - Continued working for the Czech cause in Geneva and London.

1917 - Went to Russia. Worked with the Czech National Council and helped to form the Czech Legions.

1918 - Crossed Siberia to Japan and from there to the United States. Named President of the new Czechoslovak Republic on 14 October, and left for Czechoslovakia on 20 November.

1922 - Began talks with Karel Čapek that would lead to the *Talks*.

1928 - First part of the *Talks* published.

1931 - Second part of the *Talks* published.

1935 - Resigned from the presidency in December, at the age of 85. Third part of the *Talks* and "Silence" published.

1937 - Died on 14 September.

The Talks
by Adolf Hoffmeister

SILENCE WITH
T. G. MASARYK

HOW THE TALKS CAME ABOUT

"I didn't want to lie. . ."

Many people have asked the author of *Talks with T. G. Masaryk* how the *Talks* actually took shape: did the author take them down in shorthand on the spot, did he write them up day by day? How did they come together, in other words, and how did they come about in the first place?

First of all, the author must confess that for a long time he never dreamed of recording what he had the opportunity to hear from the President's lips. Attribute it to a certain slovenliness on his part if you will, but he never carries a pad, he has never kept a diary, and his own papers and memories are a hopeless mess. I am certain you know people like him and would never expect them to maintain careful records of what they hear or see.

And then one day it rained and rained at the President's summer place in Topol'čianky, and the President and his guests were sitting around the fireplace looking at the flaming logs (the President loves to stare into the fire) and talking about this and that, when the conversation turned to the War and who had been in the worst spot when. "The worst spot I was in during the War," the President began, "was Moscow." And then he told about how he'd been sent from revolutionary Petrograd to Moscow since it was so peaceful there, and no sooner did he step off the train than he heard shooting. He headed for his hotel on foot, but was stopped outside the railway station by a cordon of soldiers who said he couldn't go any farther because of the shooting. But he got past them somehow and found himself in a square where rifles and machine guns were firing at one another, Kerensky's men on one side, the Bolsheviks on the other.

"I set off," he told us. "A man walking ahead of me suddenly broke into a run and slipped through a large door that had been opened a crack for him. It was the Hotel Metropole. I tried to slip in after him, but they slammed the door in my face. So I banged on it and shouted, 'What are you doing? Open the door!' 'Have you got a room here?' the porter shouted back. 'We can't let you in otherwise. We're all booked up.' I didn't want to lie, so I shouted, 'Stop playing games and let me in!' He was so surprised he did let me in."

He went on to describe the siege of the Metropole, the fighting in Kiev, and "our boys," as he called the Czech Legionnaires. But what struck the author of the *Talks* more than anything was that one brief phrase "I didn't want to lie." There he was — guns shooting from both sides of the square, bullets raining down on the pavement and buildings around him — there stands Professor Masaryk, and the porter won't let him in. Had he said he was staying there, the porter would have let him in immediately, but not even when his life was at stake would he let himself lie. And when he talks about it, he uses the short, dry "I didn't want to lie," meaning it goes without saying, that's all there is to it.

That was the first time the author of the *Talks* wrote down the President's words. All he wanted to do was save one brief sentence, give someone else a chance to appreciate how beautifully simple and obvious it was. It never occurred to him to go on writing down what he heard. And so it went for several years until one day — again in Topol'čianky — he was sitting and chatting with the President under some old chestnut trees (it was autumn and every once in a while the ripe, russet fruit would drop with a thud on the hard ground) when the mail came. The President got a whole stack of letters, but the author of the *Talks* got one too. From Germany. A publishing house. The Amalthea-Verlag or something of the sort. Anyway, the author of the *Talks* burst out laughing. "You know what they want?" he said to the President. "They want me to write your biography. As if I could. A biographer has to be at least something of an historian; he's got to delve into sources, check their reliability, things like that."

"True," the President nodded. "Writing a biography is hard work."

The silence that followed was broken only by the thudding and bouncing of ripe chestnuts. They reminded the author of the *Talks* of the bullets in the Moscow square and along the main thoroughfare in Kiev.

"Though I could put down the things you've told me on occasion," I blurted out. "They'd make a biography by themselves."

"Do whatever you like," he said, laughing.

"You'll help me to fill in the gaps, won't you?"

"I'll do what I can," he said, as if resigned to his fate, and got up out of his chair. "But now I've got work to do."

And that is how the *Talks* came to be written.

*

Though writing them took a good deal of doing. When the author had scribbled out everything he could remember, he found he knew quite a bit about the President's childhood (because the President enjoyed reminiscing about it and did so frequently) and a thing or two about his student years, but from then on the material was rather spotty. He would have to get the President to go on a bit about himself.

As a rule the battle was joined in the morning on the Topol'čianky grounds. At about nine the President would make his way through the meadows to his beloved arbor in the sun. The author of the *Talks* had his attack — frontal, usually — prepared in advance. He let the requisite period of silence pass and then came out with, "What was the Manuscripts Controversy* like, anyway?"

After a while the President shook his head, said "Far from pretty," and started wiping his pince-nez.

The author of the *Talks* would await further developments.

"Have you read the papers today?" the President would ask, looking up at him. "Did you notice such and such?" And then he would go on about anything and everything except the Manuscripts Controversy.

Next day the author would have another question ready. "Tell me, did you make progress in the nineties?"

"I made mistakes," the President said laconically and considered the case closed.

So you see, it wasn't easy to get the details of his life out of him, and writing the *Talks* took a good deal of patience. On both our parts.

*

Even after the author of the *Talks* had written out everything he had heard, there was still too little, still all manner of gaps. He was at a loss.

"Shall I publish it as is?" he asked one day.

"Why not?" said the President with a shrug.

"How about having a look at it," the author suggested hesitantly. "For the sake of accuracy."

"If you like," said the President. And that is how the manuscript got into his hands. By the time the author got it back, it included much new material in the President's own hand: supplementary remarks, more reminiscences, new and little known details.

Overjoyed, the author reworked his text and handed it back for revision. It was returned after a suitable interval with further additions, details, and reminiscences.

"This can't go on," he protested. "You're almost doing more work than I am."

"What's the difference?" said the President.

"Well, what about royalties?" he said, weighing the new, heavier manuscript in his hand. "We should at least split them down the middle. Fifty fifty."

The President dismissed the proposal with a wave of the hand.

"Now you've gone and done it," thought the author of the *Talks*, furious with himself. "Offering royalties to a head of state!"

But the following morning the head of state stopped short in the middle of the meadow on the way to the arbor and said, his eyes sparkling, "I know what to do with the royalties you give me! A widow I know has the sweetest, purest children. I've always meant to do something for her. I'll put this money in her name."

That too is part of the history of the *Talks*, don't you think?

TGM Not Only Talks But Is Silent

The author of the *Talks with T. G. Masaryk* is aware he would be giving the public an incomplete, even distorted image of his subject were he not to write the following chapter. Certain people have ascribed an almost photographic reality to the *Talks*. They are wrong. A photograph or, rather, a talking picture of the *Talks* would look like this: an arbor of birch wound round with climbing roses and juniper bushes; T. G. Masaryk sitting on a coarsely finished bench, his elbows on his knees, silently tugging on his mustache, completely engrossed in his thoughts. The author of the *Talks* is also silent, puffing on his pipe and engrossed in *his* thoughts, for instance, the trajectory of the ladybug crawling up his arm. Eventually the President lifts his head, waves his hand in a circle, and says, "This. . . " which means: what a day, just look at those hills on the horizon, at that maple ablaze so early. The author of the *Talks* nods wordlessly, which means: yes, simply beautiful, there's nothing finer than a brisk autumn morning, the beech trees are turning too, look, look, a squirrel, shh, you'll scare it away.

It wasn't hard to set down from memory what was said on a great many such mornings, but what can't be conveyed is the quiet, the silence the words and unhurried talk came out of. The silence was always there, slipping between words, closing sentences, but it wasn't an oppressive silence, the silence of having nothing to say; it was a thoughtful silence, the silence of a person who needs to ponder something rather than talk about it, who doesn't start talking until he's thought it through, and then talks slowly, hesitantly, translating thoughts into words. It's not easy, because words are sometimes too tight or too loose to convey thoughts. So he doesn't like to talk, and when he has to say something he says it tersely, in as few words as possible; slowly, the better to find the right words in the brooding pauses; and disjointedly because thought lacks the mechanical connections of speech. There had to be a great deal of silence for the *Talks* to come about. Only the author knows how incomplete the printed form is: it lacks the counterpoint of silence.

It is a September morning. The President is sitting in the birch arbor, hat in hand, musing. Children's shouts are coming from the

18

village, a hawk is soaring beneath the heavens, a maple leaf is sailing quietly down. The President lifts his head as if to say something, but instead merely waves a long finger in a circle and sighs, "This. . . " I know what you mean: you mean that you find it all so beautiful, that you love the sun, the ripeness of autumn, life's cheerful voice, and, most of all, that in times like these you think of God.

Right. But how to put it on paper without words?

Clearly T.G. Masaryk is not the talkative type. He is not the type that needs to talk in order to think, that thinks by means of talking or writing. A born orator is a person who comes by his ideas as he speaks, that is, his ideas stem from speech, speech having its own connections, its own flow, whisking his thought along. Masaryk is not a born orator. In his case there always seems to be a gap between thought and utterance. He finds putting thoughts into words more a burden than a relief: it forces him to abandon the flow of his ideas. Crossing the divide is tantamount to splitting himself in two: he must speak as well as think, come up with words, translate the contents of his mind into verbal constructs. It doesn't feel quite natural, it makes him insecure, the way a right-handed person feels when forced to do something with his left hand. Often he set forth a very definite idea in a rough, even sketchy manner; often he failed to finish a sentence or finished it with the wave of a hand, the shrug of a shoulder, or a vague "and the like," thereby slipping away from the flow of speech and back to the flow of thought. In grammatical terms, he often used aposiopeses (sentence fragments) and anacolutha (syntactic inconsistencies within a sentence). His punctuation is a matter of deeply pondered shreds of quiet. Don't be impatient, don't pounce on his dashes: you never know when a carefully devised word will emerge from them. A thinking man is a man of many thoughts, not of many words.

*

As I say, there is a tangible schism between thought and utterance in Masaryk. He needs only to think: he must more or less force himself to put his thoughts into words; he doesn't like to talk and finds it difficult. This makes itself felt in his speech in two ways. First, whenever possible he uses a statement he has made before, one of his own formulations. He has personal expressions, though with time he tends to shorten and condense them. These are his famous brachylogies, his mental abbreviations. Once he has thought something through and made it his own, he doesn't like going into it again in detail. That is why he encapsulates certain ready-made opinions in "ideograms." When he calls someone "an unpleasant person," for instance, the words contain a blanket condemnation of eccentrics and their way of life; they contain all the pique and indignation he can muster. The words "a decent person" are also unusually rich in meaning, implying moral integrity, common sense, reliability, courage, in short, any number of precious qualities. But the greatest praise he can give is to call someone "a beautiful person." There is an ancient, classical quality to those words.

The second consequence of Masaryk's taciturnity is just the opposite: a certain groping for words. Whereas some people make do for a lifetime with a supply of ready-made phrases, opinions, and formulations and can pull one out of the hat for every occasion, Masaryk is constantly searching for words, pausing before using them, hesitating to utter them, as though uncertain whether they fully express what he has in mind. Characteristic of the effort he puts into conveying his thoughts orally is his tendency to string together synonyms. He will say, for instance, "A state, a republic, a democracy needs such and such," where each word corroborates, delimits, and supplements the previous one. A state, yes, but a republican one; yes, a republic, but a republic that is democratic to the core; a democracy, yes, but a democracy in harmony with the state and its order. There are times when one finds a concept treated in terms of both content and scope, an attempt to define a concept together with its use. Another way of putting it would be that he thinks and speaks more in "contents" than words. By stringing words together, he wishes to bring across the breadth and depth of the content of what he has in mind.

He dislikes verbalisms; he shuns anything in speech or thought deriving from word play; he avoids similes, metaphors, analogies, and, in particular, hyperboles. He likewise dislikes such games of verbal logic as forced antitheses, conceptual dialectics, and problems provoked or resolved by words alone. Wherever he encounters them, he dismisses them with a wave of the hand and a "Mere scholasticism." Translate this into the language of politics and what do you get? Actions, not words.

He dislikes writing as much as he dislikes speaking. He once said about himself, "I'd have been satisfied to read and study, and if to write, then for myself — in short, to learn." And after an illness: "I was glad I didn't have to talk to anybody. At least I could think."

*

But when he does talk it's always with a purpose. When a new idea comes up in conversation, he will listen for a while and then say, "Such and such a book has been written on the topic," which means, "What's the point in talking when we can read?" But he loves to listen to an expert talk, an expert in anything, so long as he really knows what he's talking about. "An interesting person" is what he calls anyone who can tell him things he didn't know before. He will make himself comfortable and listen to such people with great pleasure. He will even interrogate them, and he is otherwise extremely reticent about asking questions of people (apparently he thinks of questions as intruding upon their silence). He will listen enrapt to the most technical of expositions and then say, "I liked the way he threw himself into what he was saying; I liked the brightness in his eyes."

We must never talk about what we don't know. When asked about something outside his expertise, he will invariably say, "I don't know," and he crossly qualifies as "an ignorant person" anyone who ventilates ideas and opinions on matters in which he has insufficient knowledge and experience. Masaryk has no patience with such people.

For practical reasons the *Talks* contain many more apodictic statements than he actually made. He is more likely to introduce a point with the words "I think," "the way I would put it," or "as I see it." Sometimes he doesn't respond at all; he merely gives an "I don't rightly know" shrug of the shoulders. But the following day he'll come out with, "You asked me yesterday about such and such. Well, I've given it some thought, and it's thus and so," and days later he'll come back to it: "Remember when we were talking about such and such? Well, I think I ought to add that. . ."

As I see it, everything he says belongs to one of two basic categories. The first consists of the certainties, firm principles, and truths he has settled upon. These he expresses forcefully, with uncommon terseness and brachylogical concision, emphasizing his point with a clenched fist or an energetically raised finger. The second consists of meditations, probings, the endless road to knowledge, endless criticism and self-criticism. And I can't tell which is more characteristic: the clear-cut, steadfast certainty of a man of firm knowledge and beliefs or the never-ending pursuit of truth.

*

Because that is what it all boils down to: for Masaryk, speaking means speaking the truth. And believe me: the very style of truth — the way it is expressed — differs from the style of half-truths, lies, or ignorance. Truth has nothing to hide or veil with words, it does not need to be decorated, prettied up. The word is not a garment to clothe thought; it does its best to be thought itself or at least a report on the content of thought. When Masaryk speaks, he reports on what he is thinking: he is sober, concrete, and as succinct as possible; he refuses to let the words carry him away. Normally our thoughts are fragmentary, but we talk about them in complete, coherent sentences; we say more than we actually thought. Masaryk, on the other hand, thinks his thoughts through before uttering them. The utterance must wait; it never precedes thought. The tempo, texture, and syntax of his speech are determined by the thought process. There is no verbal assembly line at work, no pyrotechnics born of verbal encounters; each sentence emerges slowly, word by word and after long intervals. Such a sentence is no formal, logical mold to pour thoughts into; it is the result of a thought clearing its own path, pausing, vacillating, then forging ahead on its own. Masaryk's sentences must be read slowly and in several breaths. Take your time with them and they will repay you not only with their full meaning but with the personal intonation and spirit of their maker.

Let me repeat that thought clears its own path in everything Masaryk says. I repeat it because the *Talks* are quite misleading in this respect. They were not so coherent as they appear: no topic was exhausted in one sitting and in the order in which it appears. Masaryk's thought follows its own path; it has its own cadence, you might say, to which it almost invariably returns. Every one of the talks eventually led to politics or God, to current events or eternity. Masaryk would lure the author of the *Talks* away from various points to these two primary ones, which seem to be constantly on his mind: they are present even if he is talking about other things, and when the opportunity arises he quietly steers the conversation back to them. This dual *terminus ad quem* is by no means self-contradictory; he remains true to himself in both, both representing a single reality but perceived now *sub specie aeterni*, now *sub specie* current events. For Masaryk, religion consists first and foremost of humanity, loving your neighbor, serving your fellow man, but politics consists of making humanity and love a reality. It is only a short step from one to the other. He never mixes the two — in his religiosity he is ever the believer, in his politics ever the politician — but the two are never in conflict; neither gains the upper hand. He is what is commonly called uncompromising, and to be as uncompromising as he is you must have principles all of a piece.

*

It is typical of his thought and means of expression that they eschew radical antitheses. Say he is talking about democracy and dictatorship. You might expect him to set one against the other, treat them as polar opposites, but no: he muses a bit and says, "Don't forget that a democracy can't do without dictatorship and a dictatorship invokes democracy." And so on down the line. He sees no conflict between theory and practice; he does not treat reason and feeling as mutually exclusive; he does not exclude the coexistence of faith and science; he does not separate politics and morality; he does not oppose body and soul; he finds no dualism between the temporal and the eternal. He brings all these artificially disconnected, polarized concepts back together, enabling them to permeate and complement one another in the single, integral, whole, and concrete reality from which they came. He stresses their wholeness, their integrity. We must accept all reality, take it as a whole: such is Masaryk's "concretism" and pluralism.

What we still need is a term to convey not only the concreteness and plenitude but also the totality, the synthesis and equilibrium, the serenity and all-encompassing, indissoluble nature — to be brief, the classical essence, to be even briefer, the harmony — of his thought. He feels no need to reconcile antitheses and bridge opposites because his system does not produce them; he feels no need to seek out a final wholeness because wholeness is his point of departure. His noetic is a noetic of the whole: he recognizes the *whole* person, with everything that person has to offer. His metaphysics is a metaphysics of the whole: he accepts the "material world and the spiritual one, the inner world of personal consciousness and the consciousness of the masses, the world of the soul, God." His commandment of love is a commandment of the whole: love fully, with all your being, love God and man, love all mankind; his humanity is universal love. The present is a piece of history; the past and the future are alive in us; we live every instant in eternity; such is the fullness and wholeness of our lives. Fullness and wholeness, again and again, at all times and in all things. A static ideal, I would say: where everything forms a whole, an aggregate, neither life nor history is a matter of constantly moving from one thing to another but of perfecting and deepening something enduring. This is what he himself terms his platonism. The main thing is not so much that there is motion as what it is that moves and changes and what endures despite the motion. And how are we to understand the element that endures even in development if not as a plan, a purposeful ideal? Development is not change, it is a process of perfection. Nor must we be thrown by misfortunes and temporary crises, for are we not at the very inception of development?

Let's say we oppose faith and science. Science denies faith and wishes to replace it with knowledge. But here Masaryk raises a monitory finger: there is science and science, faith and faith. Science denies blind faith, superstitious, unthinking faith; moreover, science can be officious, overbearing, and pseudo-scientific, claiming to know everything. True science and true faith are not mutually exclusive. How like Masaryk to say that there is no antagonism between science and faith, only between science and pseudo-science, between true, conscious faith and mechanical, idolatrous faith; there is no conflict between freedom and discipline, only between true freedom and anarchistic freedom, between slavish discipline and the discipline of mutual assistance. The list could be expanded. Human ideals never exclude one another in their ideal form, in their wholeness and perfection. By thinking things through and perfecting them, we foster their synthesis. Another classical element: there can be no conflict in fullness and wholeness. By becoming ever more familiar with reality, by guiding our actions with ever greater knowledge and love, we draw closer and closer, step by step, to the objective harmony of the world — to God's order, as Masaryk the believer puts it.

He has a curious concept of time. Should he open a conversation about politics with the words "If we look back a little in time. . ." don't expect him to talk about the early days of our Republic or about Körber. "Looking back a little in time" means going back to the Roman Empire or the medieval church. All history is an argument for today; all history is, as it were, taking place today. He refers to Plato as if the *Politics* had come out just last year and were still all the rage in political theory.

Yet time for him encompasses not only the history of mankind but its future as well. He is constantly thinking ahead: what tomorrow will bring, what things will be like ten years from now, a century or two from now. Everything we do moves history forward; we are paving the way for the future. We must therefore ask ourselves not only what history is but also where it is heading.

He has almost no memories. Like every elderly person he enjoys reminiscing about his childhood, but he would much rather look into the future. It is indicative of his metaphysical faith that he sees the entire course of the world as a progression towards something better, a process of perfection. The Golden Age does not lie behind us; it is the goal of all human efforts. We must not be impatient if we cannot reach out and touch it; we must not lose heart. God's mills grind slowly, he reminds us. If that patient, valiant hope is not true optimism, I don't know what is.

Still, nothing we can do now should be postponed: no conviction that things will be better in a few thousand years absolves us of the responsibility to do everything within our power to improve conditions today. Even if we live in eternity, we must live full, integral lives. Only by living in the here and now do we learn and love. That, we might say, is the key to Masaryk's thought.

*

Rather than provide an outline or analysis of Masaryk's philosophy, I have tried to present more or less the spiritual background or space against which the sentences and chapters of the *Talks* came into being. On the one hand, it is ten o'clock on a September morning in the year such and such and the President, having finished reading the papers, is about to embark on the duties that "go with the job" of being president. On the other, a more universal time is hovering over the birch arbor: Plato talks to us, and Augustine; whole eras, whole centuries come together; we hear measured, thoughtful deliberations on current events like the fall of the Roman Empire, the rise of such and such a world power, the liberation of the human spirit; Hus* battles for the truth, George of Poděbrady* for peace, Comenius* for education. Everything that has ever happened here at home and out in the world comes into play, just as we form our image of the day from the morning papers or as an artisan takes a look around his shop to make sure everything is in place before he sets to work. Yes, everything is in place, the history of all times, the voices of all teachers, man proposing and God disposing. And after going on for a while about this or that topic, the President starts thinking about work.

He thinks about what has to get done, about this and that concrete task, but hovering over the day-to-day political situation, which he is actively and lovingly involved in, is something like an enormous space: his all-encompassing conception of humanity and divinity, of harmony and providence. He may lose his temper, he may discourse on the events of the day, he may simply be silent — that great overriding order is always present. Sometimes what he says sounds almost dry: no big words, no fire-and-brimstone sermons, no conceptual hocus-pocus, just the facts, straight-forward definitions, concrete criticism, practical common sense. But pay close attention and you'll hear more: the vast, sweeping, radiant space above resonates with each sentence; each word is a link in a powerful system of knowledge, faith, and love, a clod of earth, a piece of a temple under construction. Each sentence can be weighed like a block of stone, but we shall fail to understand it fully if we fail to see the pillars and buttresses, the steeples and spires of the structure as a whole. Only then can we appreciate the beautiful, wise order present in even the most simple building block.

That is what is meant by "Silence with T. G. Masaryk." Let us listen less to the words than to the deep, quiet resonances, for they are the genuine content, they the whole, utter truth. Even when the topic of conversation is something as, well, pedestrian, earthbound as politics, the resonances are there. Can't you hear the din of history and the commandments of God? Together with Plato's republic and Jesus' sermon on the mount, the great hierarchy of the Church and the bustle of secular concerns, the relief of freedom and the quiet tenacity of reason. The resonances it takes to make harmony! Reading Masaryk, reading him harmonically, involves both talk and silence: talk about the temporal world so crucial to us and silent contemplation of the eternal. Anyone who fails to contemplate the latter will have failed to understand Masaryk fully.

Talks with
T. G. Masaryk

Book One
YOUTH

CHILDHOOD

Home

My earliest memories . . . No more than disjointed images actually. Once — I must have been about three — I saw a runaway horse in Hodonín go galloping down the street. Everyone jumped out of its way except a little child, who fell under its hoofs, but the horse leaped over him and he wasn't hurt. That remains fixed in my mind. Then I remember that in those days my father would snare crows and other birds in Mutěnice and I'd go to the Mutěnice schoolmaster, ask him for pencil-ends and paper, and scribble with them before I learned to write.

My home was the countryside around Hodonín. It was all Imperial Estates then, and wherever my father was sent — he began his working life as a coachman on the Estates — we moved with him. When I was only two, we moved from Hodonín to Mutěnice, where we lived until the spring of 1853; then we went back to Hodonín and lived in a cottage on a lake. I can still see that broad plain, and the impression it made on me as a child seems to have had its effect: I love the plains. I like mountains from a distance, but I don't like living in them: valleys hem me in and there's so little sunshine.

In 1856 we moved to a farm in Čejkovice. Two years later we had to go to Čejč for a year, then back to Čejkovice, and there we lived until 1862. In 1862 I started attending the *Realschule* or secondary school in Hustopeč and my parents returned to Hodonín, but in 1863 they were sent back to Čejč, and three years later — in 1867 — they left the Imperial Estates and went into private service in Miroslav on a farm called Suchohrdly or, in German, Socherle. They spent the longest period, from 1870 to 1882, in Klobouky, which is where I spent my holidays. But my real childhood home was Čejkovice.

Mother had more influence on me than Father. Father was gifted but simple; Mother ruled the roost. She was originally from Haná, but had grown up among Germans in Hustopeč, so Czech was hard for her at first. She was awfully fond of her three young rascals. I may have been her pet, but the one who really deserved it was my brother Martin, the best, the purest of the three, an *anima candida*, a bright soul.

Mother was an intelligent woman and wise; she knew something of the world and had lived for some time "in society," if only as a servant: she had been cook for a gentleman's family in Hodonín. They were fond of her there and later came to her for advice and aid in hard times. It was living with them that made her want to see her children rise a bit on the social scale, and she was well acquainted with the wretched conditions the working and serving classes lived in at the time. She wanted to turn us children into gentlefolk, and it was thanks to her I was sent to school.

Mother was a religious woman. She loved going to church, though she hardly ever found time for it: she had to slave for the family. "Herrendienst geht vor Gottesdienst," she would say. Serve your master before you serve your God. I'd remember that later when I came to understand the political role played by the Church and Feuerbach's theory that religion serves political ends. Instead of going to church, Mother would say her prayers from a prayer book. It was full of pictures. I remember one of the crucified Christ spouting blood. That was her favorite. I couldn't take my eyes off it either.

Father was a Slovak from Kopčany. He was born a serf and a serf he remained all his life. Unlike Mother he had little positive influence on me. Nature gave him many gifts, but he never went to school. In Kopčany he learned to read a little from an old woman, a soldier's widow the parish had asked to serve as teacher (Kopčany had no school of its own); in exchange for reading lessons the children dug up potatoes for her. So he was altogether a man of the country rather than the town, a man of nature. He always lived close to nature, especially after starting to farm. He understood nature, observed it closely and well, and had a special sense for the fine points of country life. I still remember how one day he brought home a young March hare snuggled in his coat — he'd

31

found it crouching in a horse's hoofprint — and gave us a lively, detailed account of its entire life.

Although he himself had no schooling, he was all for my education and wasn't ashamed to study with me. Of course he viewed his studies, like everything else, in a utilitarian light: what mattered was what they would bring him. He wasn't religious, but he was afraid of hell, and now and then he went to church on Sundays. Mother made all the decisions; he gave in even when he didn't agree with her.

When he came to see us in Prague much later, the only thing he cared about was the way the horses were shod and the kinds of shafts, axles, and wheels the carts and carriages had. All he found interesting in Malá Strana's palaces was the porters: he got to know them in no time and always went to chat with them. After two or three days, though, he'd have had enough of Prague and nothing we could do would make him stay. He needed to go home, to the village, to nature.

I could see and feel the effect of subjugation and enforced servitude on Father. He did his duty without pleasure, because he had to; he doffed his hat to his masters, but felt no affection for them. Serfdom continued to exist *de facto* on the Imperial Estates even after 1849. Believe it or not, my father had to ask for permission to send me to secondary school. My first impressions of the social order consisted of watching officials on the estate be rude to my father. I often wondered how to get back at them, give them a good hiding. When the masters came for the hunt, they'd leave their fur coats at our house. Oh, how I longed to vent my boyish rage on those coats. After the hunt they'd have a meal at the gamekeeper's cottage and the servants tossed the leftovers to the villagers, who fought over them. Once it was something that must have been macaroni. The villagers, not knowing what it was, called it "worms," and still they fought over it like beasts.

These are the sorts of things that remain fixed in my mind.

Children on Their Own

We three brothers were very fond of one another, but I had a different relationship with each. Martin, the middle brother (we were each two years apart), I more than loved; you might say I revered him. He was so dear, so trusting, forthright, unassuming. The youngest, Ludvík, I tended to order about: I had him run my errands and so on. I still think of Martin as an ideal boy.

My brothers weren't my friends; we each went our own way. My friends came from the older boys; I've always liked being with people older than I am, listening to them. I was even on friendly terms with one or two of the local grooms.

*

Anyway, I started school in Hodonín — a German school — and went on in Čejkovice. I can still see the hands of my first Čejkovice schoolmaster — hairy, bony hands always cuffing us. Father learned to write from me at home. While he was a coachman, he didn't need to write, but later, when he became a bailiff and an independent farmer, he needed to keep records of work and workers — what they did and how many hours they put in. I always helped him with them, drawing lines in his notebook and making the necessary columns. My father didn't care for work, you see. Like any indentured servant he worked only when he had to. That's what being indentured means: having to do what you don't want to.

When I was young, a village schoolmaster was terribly poor, his salary so small he eked it out with various kinds of clerical work and church jobs — singing at funerals, caroling at Christmas. At vintage time we boys would go from one wine press to another, collecting new wine in a barrel for our teacher, asking each farmer to pour in as much as he could. The teacher would keep the barrel behind the school stove all winter (he had no cellar), and there the fermentation would take place. He was really little better than a beggar, and a farmer — especially if he happened to be a council member or mayor — treated him like one. It goes without saying that the poor slave of a schoolmaster had little authority over the children, so he walloped and walloped them, the switch being his chief educational tool. A slave always uses a slavedriver's methods and takes his revenge where he can.

Now you see how far today's schools have come. Yet there is still much that needs reforming if they are to turn out independent, self-confident individuals with pluck and spirit. School reform is also, properly speaking, teacher and teaching reform, which means raising the teacher's social status and level of education. Nowadays teachers themselves are demanding higher education, and we must look into how the more academically trained teacher relates to children. The chief attributes of a good teacher are a love of children; the ability to think and feel one's way into their inner lives, which are more concrete and image-oriented than abstract and scientific; the ability to make lessons graphic, pin the object of a lesson to something the children can actually see in their surroundings; and the ability to make instruction as individual as possible. Far more thought should be given to education and teaching and far more funding granted them than has been the case. The development of democracy is closely tied to the development of education.

*

You have no idea the things a country boy has to know! Start counting, all right? He's got to be able to whistle with his lips, between his teeth, with one finger or two, and with his fist; he's got to know two ways of snapping his fingers; he's got to know all kinds of ways to fight and how to stand on his head, walk on his hands, and turn cartwheels, and how to run — that's most important of all. (Our favorite game was called "battering ram" and involved hopping up and down with your arms crossed in front of you while ramming into your opponent's shoulder with your own and causing him to lose his balance and lower his raised leg. We usually played one on one, but sometimes three, four, and even a pack of boys would go at it together.) Then he's got to be able to shoot with slings and bows, throw a stone accurately, ride a horse, crack both whips and switches, climb any tree, catch crayfish and beetles, swim, kindle a fire, slide, toboggan, hold his own in a snowball fight, walk on stilts, and umpteen other things. Once we started digging a tunnel to run a train through, and where we were going to find the train didn't bother us in the slightest.

Still counting? Because a boy's occupations also include making twig or quill popguns, carving whistles out of willow sprigs or goose bones and clarinets out of cherry wood, making pipes from the stems of wheat or pumpkin vines, bows (or perhaps even crossbows) from a shingle block and arrows to go with it, and rifles, swords, and shakos, balls and bats, toy starlings and fleas, toy windmills and watermills, and even the odd Easter rattle; he must be able to tie Gordian knots and braid rings and whole chains out of horsehair (it was a German boy on an exchange visit to our village who taught us that), and the only tool he has for it all is a cheap jackknife. To have a bona fide pocket knife is every boy's fondest dream, and every boy who can borrows a file or chisel or ax from home and carves and carpenters away. Every boy has a bit of the engineer in him.

Once there was nothing in the world I wanted more than a Jew's harp. A Jew's harp is a musical instrument played by gypsies and shaped like a small lyre. It has a metal tongue you blow on and twang with your finger. Anyway, I longed to have one and asked a gypsy to make one for me. "All right," said the gypsy, "but I'll need some iron first." So I brought him a piece of iron I'd found on the farm. "And now some bread." So I gave him some bread and then butter and eggs — I don't know what I didn't give him! And I never did see the Jew's harp.

We knew any number of games. We were anything but pacifists in our war games, playing "soldiers." We also played "robbers." I was chief of the robber band, and the son of the estate's steward was chief of police. You can be sure I gave him a good drubbing whenever I got the chance.

A boy always has a treasure box filled with colored beans, buttons, peacock and jay feathers, cubes of tile shards, colored glass, a prism or lens from a chandelier (a church chandelier, perhaps), and other such riches. Boys have their business deals as well, lending out beans at high interest and sometimes even selling them for a kreutzer.

Before tending to all these boyish activities, of course, a country boy had to help his mother at home and his father in the fields. I can't say what sort of life the girls lived, since we had nothing to do with them: boys and girls lived quite separate lives. Once, when I was eight or so, my mother took me with her on a pilgrimage to Šaštín. We slept at the house of a gamekeeper friend of the family, and he and his wife had a girl about my age. We spent two days there, and the girl and I played together from morning till night. Back home I missed her terribly.

City boys have fewer varieties of games; maybe scouting takes up the slack nowadays. Children should be allowed to kick up a bit of a storm. A child brought up in the country is more resourceful, independent, and practical; a city child can scarcely sharpen his own pencil and has no way of learning to use his hands. Surprisingly few accidents take place in the country. A few sprained ankles from time to time, and a stone in the head, true. But I can remember only three serious accidents: one boy fell from fairly high in a poplar and apparently did some permanent harm to his chest; another was poisoned with henbane when the boys he was playing "horses" with fed him "poppies"; and a third drowned while swimming in the lake. I was there when they brought him home, and I saw his mother kneel down and keen him in long drawn-out tones, extolling all his fine qualities: "Oh, my beautiful little Josef, what a good boy you were. I'll never scold you again" and so on. Later I read that this kind of lamenting and praising the dead is customary among all primitive peoples.

Children can always tell whether their parents and grandparents are free and how they feel about one another. American children are freer than European children; they're more naive and open in their ways among themselves and with adults. They don't fear adults; they see that adults too are open with one another. That's what comes of living in a free country, a republic. People don't lie; they're not constantly afraid of being cheated or hurt by one another, they're not afraid of one another, period. I like watching our children, talking to them. They seem more spirited and open even now, and I'm sure they'll grow into free people. Let me tell you, a republic is a mighty fine thing!

Which brings me back to the issue of schools and teachers. All teachers have an obligation to impress the principles of republicanism, democratic freedom, and equality on their pupils; they should be friends with their pupils. Their authority should rest entirely on their difference in age and their superiority in matters of knowledge, practice, and character. According to my observations, American children are on much more friendly terms with their teachers than our children and have pleasant memories of their teachers and schools. Our children heave a sigh of relief when they leave school, and yet learning, getting to know things, is a joy for the normal child. American teachers play football with their pupils without fear of losing face, while our teacher-bureaucrats would never dream of going tobogganing or skating with their pupils: the first tumble might cost them their dignity or authority. We've put the same artificial distance, the same barrier between teacher and pupil as we have between official and citizen. You need more life and more heart for a real democracy. Our Comenius* considered school the *officina humanitatis*, the workshop of humanity. School trains the collective as well as the individual or, rather, it trains the individual for society and democracy. I'd like to see old songs like "O ancient Czechs! O valiant Czechs" give way to songs that go "O pedagogues! Be democrats!" One of our strengths is that even now we have a few who are.

The same holds for the family, of course: instead of blind parental authority and passive obedience induced by never-ending tongue-lashings and dressings-down, what we need is training by example.

The Child and His World

Like my mother I was deeply religious. I was server to the Čejkovice chaplain Father František (Satora his name was), and I absolutely adored him. I loved his white collar and that tight-fitting black — what do you call it? — cassock, the gown with little round buttons running from neck to feet. When I served Mass, Father Satora was like God and I was his angel and oh so happy. Much happier than when singing in the choir. I was also very proud of my own cassock.

Father Satora, a Slovak from Boršice near Uherské Hradiště, was a curious man, a split personality. At times he was a real fanatic, but he also seemed tormented by doubt. He was not in the good graces of either the ecclesiastical or the worldly authorities. At one point I heard the local women whispering about him and the schoolmaster's wife, who had just had a baby. I racked my brains for an explanation. Then one Sunday he preached a sermon about how even a priest is prone to sin and the congregation must not take example from his life but from Christ and the words he taught them. It was a public confession that I could not understand at the time, but it gave me great pause. Why shouldn't people take example from his life? Only much later, looking back over my life, did I understand this and much else.

As time went on and I read and experienced more, I came to think more critically about priests, and eventually it dawned on me that there is a difference between religion and the Church. Even secondary-school catechists admit that while the Church is a divine institution, it has certain human attributes, attributes which, because they are insubstantial and mutable, vary according to nation and country. And although I've been increasingly involved in this human side of things, I've never harbored any doubts about God and theology; I've always been an optimist.

At the time I was unable to imagine that another faith could exist. Then I ran across an article about Russia in an old almanac. It included something on the Orthodox Church. You can't imagine how disturbed I was by the news that there was another religion like ours with its own pilgrimages, hermits, saints, and miracles. I was impressed by the argument that there are more Catholics than Protestants and Orthodox Christians, but upset to learn that there are even more Mohammedans and heathens.

I also heard that there were Protestants — Calvinists — as nearby as Klobouky, so I made my own reconnaissance pilgrimage there and sneaked into the Evangelical Chapel. I was terribly afraid of falling down dead or being struck by lightning as a punishment, but nothing happened. The bare walls, the pulpit that took the place of the altar, and the stark, serious atmosphere — it all took my breath away. I'd heard people reproach the Protestants for not believing in bells, but in those days Protestant churches were not permitted to have them. It wasn't until a hundred years after Joseph II's Patent of Toleration that they were granted the right to ring bells. I was shocked Catholics should admit that Protestants were more cultured, more methodical, and more thrifty than they were. How could that be? I wondered. I also wondered why people said, "It lasts like the Calvinist faith." And because I found no solutions to my riddles, I continued to be disturbed and somehow provoked by Protestantism.

As for Judaism, well, I was afraid of Jews: I believed they use Christian blood in their rituals. I would go several streets out of my way to avoid Jewish houses. Jewish children wanted to play with me because I knew a little German, but I refused. It was only later, at the Hustopeč school, that I more or less made my peace with the Jews. Once on a school trip to the Pálavské Hills we were cavorting about after our meal at the tavern when I saw one of our Jewish schoolmates slip away. I was curious and followed him. He was kneeling behind an open gate with his face to the wall, praying. For some reason I felt ashamed to see a Jew praying while we played. I was loath to admit that he prayed as fervently as we did and had remembered to say his prayers even in the midst of our frolic.

Anyway, all my life I've gone out of my way not to be unjust to Jews. That's why I've been said to favor them. When did I get over my "folk" anti-Semitism? Well, maybe never on an emotional level, only rationally. After all, it was my own mother who taught me the superstition about Jews' making use of Christian blood.

As a child, of course, I didn't believe only the things we were taught at school and in church: my Catholicism was shot through with superstition and Moravian-Slovak mythology. I believed in all possible and impossible spirits and particularly in the "midday crone" and the "evening crone" who carry off naughty children. That was because I would lose track of time when I was out playing and come home late for the midday and evening meals. The *hastrman*, our freshwater merman, was especially popular among my playmates; nearly everybody claimed to have seen one, but there were great disputes over what he looked like, what color hair, beard, and clothes he had. Witches were high on our lists as well, and Death and the Devil. We all heard the latter in church when a man had an epileptic fit during Mass one day. I also worried about black priests or wizards after reading about them. In other words, I lived in a kind of dualistic spiritual world that might be called simultaneously orthodox and unorthodox. The unorthodox world — a world of superstitions and anthropomorphisms (or, rather, pedomorphisms) — had no system to it: the evening crone and the hastrman and all the other monster-like beings were separate from one another, unconnected. I thought it strange and even knew they were superstitions, but I couldn't make out the boundary between superstition and faith, and they were so firmly rooted and widely accepted I couldn't help believing in them. Not even the priest who taught us our catechism in school dared to deny them. I can say that the midday crone is actually the eerie silence of the noonday hour and that the evening crone is the twilight, but a child's mind clings to its "pedomorphisms": a child loves the poetry of myths. Of course, the child is soon weaned from such poetry. One day I would get home after the evening bells and be told the evening crone would get me; the next I'd be told to stay out late in the fields and watch over the potatoes. If I said I was afraid, they'd laugh at me: "Listen to him! The evening crone!"

Neither at school nor at home was there any serious talk of the spiritual essence of religion; I never heard that religion was something a person could or should meditate on. The religion of the people, like its symbols and the entire cult, was extremely material, objective, objectivistic. It never occurred to anyone that religion might have subjective elements to it. Religion was the truth of God revealed; it was the commandment of God and the Church; it was, as Vincent of Lerinum put it in his classic formulation: *quod semper, quod ubique, quod ab omnibus creditum est,* what was always and everywhere believed by everyone. The only things I ever speculated on in those days were such extrinsic matters as whether the emperor or the pope was the greater sovereign. When I came up against the Holy Trinity, the incarnation of God in a human body, and other such dogmas I couldn't understand, I would ask Father Satora about them, but I had to accept the standard answer: they were mysteries. That may have ended the discussion, but it didn't satisfy me. Religion was something to be lived and practiced, church doctrine something to be accepted. All we knew of the Bible we learned from what we read in schoolbooks and what we heard in church. We never read the Bible at home; all we read was the prayer book, and that only occasionally.

A groom at the castle once hanged himself in the stable, and when I was shown the gate he'd hung from, it so terrified me that I never crossed the threshold of that stable again. How could you take your own life? It was so frightening, so incomprehensible. Taking your own life was unnatural, perverse! I couldn't get it out of my mind, especially later, when I found a book about people who managed to hold out under the most hair-raising circumstances. It told about a monk, for instance, who was buried in a crypt but only appeared to be dead, and he had either to keep himself going until a new funeral set him free or else kill himself. Well, for twenty years he lived buried alive, feeding on insects that fell through a little window in the crypt and licking the moisture of the walls and tombs. I couldn't help wondering what happened in winter, when there are no insects, but the casuistry of the story and others like it held me in its thrall and impressed the issue of voluntary death on my brain. My book on suicide was a response to that boyhood experience and later experiences as well.

*

Prague? Bohemia? I knew nothing of them at the time. For the Slovaks in my region there was only one city: Vienna. People from our parts went to Vienna to study and work, and every once in a while we had smartly dressed Viennese visitors. Once there was a butcher's journeyman in Hungarian dress with spurs on his boots and a hatchet-top cane. When he went to church, his spurs made such a racket that everybody stared at him. A pity he had only one eye: it didn't go with the rest of his get-up. A Viennese Slovak tried getting us to believe that Vienna has an india-rubber bridge that sways whenever anyone walks or rides on it. We nicknamed Czechs "golden gentlemen" because they called everybody "my golden one." I first heard of Prague from a book entitled *A Child's Heritage*, which described a family driving its cart into Prague and then the beauties of the city itself.

I thought of myself as Slovak. My Kopčany grandmother would bring me floppy white Slovak trousers as a present, but I wore town clothes. When I went off to school in Hustopeč, my parents had a suit made from my father's old coachman's livery. It was blue with brass buttons. You should have seen the boys laugh at me.

I considered Hodonín a metropolis because its church had a steeple while the Čejkovice church had only a belfry. I got to know Hustopeč quite early too: my mother's people lived there. Once I went to the Hustopeč fair. My uncle gave me six whole kreutzers, and I bought a paintbox with them: little cakes of paint and a brush in a wooden container, a real treasure. On the way home we got caught in a storm; the rain beat down in torrents. I stuck the paintbox under my arm, then under my coat, and finally under my shirt. When I got home, I had paint all over my clothes and skin. So I didn't become a painter. For some reason I didn't do well in painting at school; I was better at drawing. Later, at the Brno Gymnasium, I enjoyed technical drawing, which was given as an elective course by our mathematics teacher, Professor Adam. I was a pretty good mathematician, and he would take my part at staff meetings when I had run-ins with other teachers.

A Year in the Country

Thinking back on it now, I can only marvel at the number of impressions a country child collects! In winter you had Saint Nicholas and the Devil. The Devil is an extremely influential personage, and even while teaching at the University I played Saint Nicholas for my children. Then there was Christmas and its carols. Every Christmas a man would appear out of nowhere with a model of the Manger in Bethlehem. It was a show for the whole village. After that came the Three Kings and the Lenten masquerades. A child always had something to look forward to. But most fun of all were the plucking parties, when as many as twenty people gathered round a table — and tongues wagged! We children would pinch and nudge one another so as not to fall asleep and miss any of the ghost stories — or the cakes that made the rounds at the end.

At the first sign of spring we would kick off our shoes. There was still ice on the ground, but we raced around barefoot. And the moment the ground was dry, the bat-and-bean season began. (A ball that had enough india rubber to bounce on the ground or off a wall was a great rarity. That made india rubber a precious commodity, and whoever came across a piece cut it off and turned it into a ball.) Soon it was Eastertime and we'd run around with Easter rattles, and on Easter Monday we'd slash at the girls with braided willow switches and sing Easter songs for Easter eggs. Resurrection was a great holiday as well, the greatest of all in Hodonín, because two dragoons with unsheathed swords would stand watch on either side of God's grave. I couldn't take my eyes off them.

Then in May we had processions through the fields, litanies for crops, and "visitations," when priests from the whole region met together with the dean for a banquet and cooks baked and fried a whole week in advance and we altar boys served at table. Or there'd be a fire in the village. That too is a holiday for a boy. We'd be at school and at the first sound of a bell or trumpet we leaped out of the windows and the girls rushed out of the doors. (Our schoolroom had a Dutch stove we'd removed a few tiles from, so we could also slip out through the gap.) Now and then a boy took a holiday on his own, that is, he played truant. My brother Martin did it all the time, and we'd have to hunt all over Čejkovice for him. But a boy playing truant perceives the silence around him as eerie, almost depressing, because the rest of his playmates are on their benches at school.

Soldiers riding through the village represented another great event, as did raising the maypole at Whitsuntide. We boys always tried to climb it. At Whitsuntide the older boys chose leaders, a boy and a girl, to go through the village from house to house, gleaning what they could: fowls, cakes, wine. Sometimes itinerant acrobats would come and stretch a rope across the village green for their antics. We boys would imitate them afterwards, walking along the tops of garden walls, gables, or even the church roof. A fall from there would have meant "forever and ever amen" — only we didn't fall.

A funeral is a special kind of village holiday, particularly if there's a brass band. The more citizens — and especially "citizenesses" — who gathered for the event, the greater the communal feeling — and the greater the excuse to leave off work and have a good chat. We formed a parish together with the village of Podvorov, and when a funeral came from there the pallbearers would set down the coffin in front of the cross in the churchyard and go off to the inn across the road to "have a warm up" while the dean or priest was putting on his vestments. One of them had to wait outside for the reverend gentlemen to appear, after which they would gulp down their last drops and pick up the coffin. In the meantime we altar boys were standing around freezing and wondering how much we were likely to get out of it. Four kreutzers was the most we could hope for, and if they gave us only one we'd be annoyed and make our feelings known with pointed remarks.

Autumn meant bonfires and grape-picking. Then came jam-making — days and nights of stirring plums over the fire. There wasn't a lot of talking, but we did get to lick the spoon. When the potatoes were being dug, I sometimes had to watch over them till dark — I, who, as you'll remember, was so afraid of the evening crone. We didn't bother to guard fruit; there was no reason to; we picked it while it was still green. Back then, fruit trees were nothing but a burden on farmers. Fruit wasn't even considered food; we had to wait for the scientists and their vitamins for that.

On the other hand, vineyards were guarded carefully and watchmen carried guns. Maybe that's what tempted us to go after grapes. About twenty of us would gang together to outwit the watchman. Operations were always led by boys who had grapes growing at home. Stolen fruit tastes sweetest, as they say. Of course, the minute I got home my parents knew what I'd been up to. Father would take a rope and dip it in water to make it sting more, and although Mother always managed to ward off the punishment in time, the following day the watchman would come to school and point to this boy and that boy and that one. No excuse was acceptable. We all had to stretch out on the bench while the schoolmaster or the priest — yes, the priest! — gave us our twenty-five lashes.

How finely and richly nature and religion divide up the country year. All life is more of a ritual in the country than in the city; it is set in a religious frame, and the many pagan remnants do not change matters. Customs have an institutional character to them; they regulate life, give it order. Country folk tend to shun anyone who disturbs the natural order. There was an unwritten law, for instance, that every family should make its own bread. That meant getting up at three in the morning to mix the dough in the kneading trough — which is hard work! — then heating up the oven and raking out the ashes, then baking the bread and (with it or just after it) flat cakes — you know, the ones that taste so good spread with dripping. And any housewife who bought her bread instead of baking it was literally held in contempt by the others. Nowadays I believe almost everyone in our villages buys bread; in other words, even in the countryside the old order is changing. Sundays also give life a ritual-like rhythm, and I continue to keep the Sabbath.

As I grew more mature, I began making a conscious study of country ways. While a student at the University of Vienna, I spent my holidays in Klobouky outside Brno and thought of writing a village novel. The local doctor, an interesting fellow, was going to be my hero, the central figure in a chronicle of country life. Not long ago I came across a few pages of that early attempt. I later spent my holidays in Bystrička and there too observed the way a village lives from year to year. If our doctors, priests, and teachers had the desire and the skill to observe country life, the wealth of material they'd come up with! A group of pastors in Germany has recently published a report of their findings; we are still without anything of the sort. At least we have the works of novelists like Holeček, Baar, Herben, the Mrštíks, Teréza Nováková, and Šoltésová. Today village life is undergoing profound changes, but present-day writers don't seem interested. Heavens! With all that unexplored life in our villages and towns!

Not only a farmer's life but life itself is regulated by the climate, the alternation of hot and cold weather, and even by the sun or, rather, the relationship of the earth to the sun. Oddly enough, people think less about the sun than about the moon, yet the moon shines only thanks to the light it borrows from the sun. Of course, you can't look at the sun the way you can look at the moon, and it's less intriguing: it shines all the time and is always the same, whereas the moon is full for only a brief interval and is constantly changing shape. People are strange, strange and superficial. Then again, night has a special significance for people, and some of its prestige rubs off on the moon: there are more Czech folk songs about the moon than about the sun, I believe, the "little moon" and "little sun," as we like to call them. Germans and many other peoples lack our diminutives.

Childhood and Education

Here's how I see it in a nutshell: The child's first and most important school is the family, and the family trains the child less by what it says or commands — we Czechs do far too much preaching, even in the home — than by what it shows, that is, what the child observes. The greatest influence on the child is what his parents are like, their relationship to each other and to their surroundings. Think of it: if a child sees his parents quarreling all the time, being coarse and disrespectful, telling lies, how — without a superhuman effort — can he grow into a decent person? The old saw "What you cook in the pot leaves its smell" applies likewise to the family.

Equally important is the way children of different ages relate to one another. I don't think it's good to be an only child. Siblings observe the natural law of seniority, the older sibling taking the lead, the younger one following or at least pretending to. Then there is the brother-sister relationship, the older brother protecting his sisters, the older sister practically mothering her younger siblings. Relationships among children are thus a pre-configuration of the adult world.

Next you have relatives, godparents, neighbors, and their influence, which taken as a whole represents the educational influence of the clan. The old order — the extended family or clan — has passed away, but its traditions live on in another, freer form and affect the child's development. The more intimate circle of relatives are the first people a child comes into contact with and observes — sometimes all too well. My favorite was my uncle, a baker in Hustopeč, who, rough though he could be (he beat his wife and children), was basically a reliable, sensible, hardworking man. He was a Slovak from Cáhnov, a Germanized village at the time, and I couldn't help wondering what it took to turn a Slovak into a German. Later, during one of my Gymnasium holidays, I looked in on my Cáhnov relatives to observe how the change took place.

The influence of the school goes beyond the didactic to the moral. Children see through the teacher if he is coarse, unfair, or lazy; they see how he behaves with his superiors — the school inspector, for instance, the mayor, the dean of the church — and what they see influences their character and moral convictions. Then there is the influence of their schoolmates, a whole new mix of familial and social factors. Our schools were coeducational out of financial necessity: one room for all, but boys on one side, girls on the other — two separate worlds.

Then a child finds a friend, someone he spends all his time with, tells his most intimate thoughts to, models himself after. Friends change with the years, as if complementing and correcting that first choice.

The collections of books and objects at a child's school are a real revelation to him. Father Satora would give me books — mostly translations from Nieritz and volumes from the Heritage series — but there was no such thing as a collection of natural objects. Not until the *Realschule* did I find something resembling a physics laboratory, and it was then I started collecting insects and pressed flowers. Think what it means for a child to get to know his own region through collections of minerals, plants, and stuffed birds and mammals. Of course, teaching materials like these and school libraries cost money, as does having decent and decently staffed schools (in my time there was no such thing as a schoolmistress) in every village. But the money must be found and allotted to them.

Ad vocem books for children; we pride ourselves on being the nation of Comenius, yet we have a dearth of children's literature and even less *good* children's literature. I've given a lot of thought to what causes the failing. Because it's a moral failing as well. Most of our children's literature consists of dull moralizing. Its authors manage to write in a popular, chatty vein, but they lack psychological insight into the child's mind: they fail to understand how truthful and sensible a child is despite its naïveté; they fail to appreciate the child's interests and outlook. I'm always embarrassed when I'm visiting somewhere and the children address me not in their own words but in lofty, pretentious phrases placed in their mouths by adults, phrases they would never dream of uttering themselves. Our children's literature makes it clear that much as we fuss over our children we don't yet love them enough.

Anyway, all these influences — from family to school to books — have their effect on the development of the child. The number of factors involved! Reforming education does not simply mean perfecting teaching techniques; it means reforming the very way we adults live. We are the soil new generations grow out of: whether they are better and happier depends largely on us. That minister from Saxony was right when he told a visiting delegation of educationalists, "My concern is not to educate children; it is to educate adults."

Then there's the perennial money question. Look at education and health from the point of view of educating handicapped children or less gifted children or neglected children; anyone will tell you that good schools save money on prisons, hospitals, and poorhouses. But good education, like good teaching, must be as individualized as possible, and although we are moving in that direction I would see us go even farther. The trouble is, nothing costs more than individualization.

Or take social problems. Children are the most horrendous reminder of poverty. Being poor means more than not having enough to eat or wear; it means dreadful living conditions. It's not so bad in summer, but in winter! Whole families, large families crowded into one room. Think of the intimate, often harrowing experiences and how much deeper and more momentous they are than the schoolmaster's abstract lessons or the priest's Sunday sermons. Social problems are also problems of education.

Or take health. I can't understand why we've thought so little about playgrounds, swimming pools, and parks for children. The poorer the district, the more such facilities are needed: poor districts have more children. With the proper watering we can have the same grassy playgrounds as England. Here again it's a question of money, yet putting money into children is the best investment there is. True, there's a difference between town and country: the whole countryside is the village child's playground.

Besides all this we have the problems of pedagogy: how and what to teach. I'm glad to say a lot of thought is being devoted to it. Let's take religion first. Even as a boy I found it ridiculous to get a mark for religion. What was it, anyway? A mark for the way you reeled off your catechism. That's not religion. What we call "religion" might as well be called "school" or not even "school" but "life." We live in a time that is clearly a time of transition: we're going through a profound religious crisis. Skepticism and religious apathy (the true non-believer is indifferent rather than skeptical) are bound to have an effect on children. The crisis is universal and reaches into the home: the father tends to be less religious than the mother, which gives a boy the impression that religion is something for women and children, so he shakes it off as he grows older. Moreover, in school children receive many more scientific explanations than religious ones even if their teachers are not actively anti-clerical, and this outlook, this thorough, self-consistent scientific knowledge, will lead them to religious doubt. The historical process known as the conflict between science and faith, the battle between science and religion is currently underway in the schools and thus in the minds and hearts of our youth. I myself experienced it with great intensity, though without turmoil; many, many others think of their schooling as a time of deep crisis.

Non-denominational schools, where they exist, exclude religion from the curriculum, but a knowledge of the Old Testament is basic to the cultural heritage of every European. Nor can I imagine a Czech growing up ignorant of Jesus and his teachings. Anyone unversed in what Christianity stands for is a stranger to our cultural soil. How can you understand European history and traditions without a knowledge of the essence and evolution of the Church? The problem is how to teach it — finding the proper angle from which to appraise the historical facts — and that is a real problem for the schools. If I keep stressing this, it is because I consider religion a basic element of spiritual life and culture and regard not only religious instruction and instruction about religion but the whole issue of religious practice as one of the great unresolved issues in education.

I hear and even see that our schools have made great progress in bringing art to their pupils. We have beautifully illustrated primers and readers. Now what we need is a good and well illustrated children's literature so that children will take from school a living need for art. In my day the schoolmaster taught us to play the fiddle and we sang — mostly church music. That was something at least. Today teachers complain about being pressed for time; there is more material to cover and art education is the first to go. My feeling is that if you come up with better teaching methods you'll have more time for art.

In the country, where I grew up, education was a much simpler and more primitive operation than it is now. Country children were not (and are not even today) subjected to the myriad impressions city children receive. And although the countryside is changing rapidly and growing more and more urban in character, the process is uneven: Slovakia and Ruthenia, for example, have remained much more countrified than Bohemia, and a perspicacious cultural policy must take such differences into account.

Even as a child I would hear that the country is more healthful than the town both physically and morally, and later I became acquainted with the socialists' negative views of urban life. My own experience has been that the town and even the big city are no worse morally than the country and need not have a pernicious moral influence on the child. Even hygienically speaking, the town is no worse than the city: just compare country and city children and you'll see. The urban dweller has relatively better medical treatment and greater opportunities for physical culture in the form of sports and Sokol* drills. Given the rapid urbanization of the countryside, modern physical education techniques are every bit as necessary there as in the city. This is a complex issue, one that government and public officials must take into account.

As for the issue of morality, I find it differs in the country and the city. The country is simpler than the city in all respects and hence in matters of morality and immorality: morality in the country is deeper, in the city more sophisticated. I doubt the country is more moral than the city in terms of sexual mores. The things written about such matters in fiction betray a superficial view of both city and country life. Moreover, there is a body of scholarly literature on the subject that bears out my opinion. Another issue education must deal with.

I would also point out that parents and teachers not only educate children, they are educated by them. Looking after a child with love and concern teaches the adult a great deal, and if we taught our children freer, more democratic habits — in manners and behavior, say — we'd eventually learn them ourselves.

As I say, things are no longer as they were when I was a boy. Our society is more highly differentiated: besides the farmers I grew up with we have industrial workers and industrialists, we have more and more people with an academic background and — what is completely new — more and more people with money. Alongside socialist theories we find an attempt to construct an agrarian philosophy. Moreover, industry and technology have introduced the American ideal of efficiency. These are all major developments with a direct bearing on education and the school.

There is a lot of work being done now in the fields of child psychology and pedagogical psychology: we have books about the aptitudes of children and young adults, about educational testing, about mental and physical handicaps among children, about juvenile delinquency. True, it's all in its infancy, but the increased attention is in itself a sign of progress.

What we need most of all, however, is to give our children more love. Not by telling them we love them but by showing them, that is, by taking better care of them, living with them more. This holds particularly for fathers. How often have we seen fathers raking in the money to "give their children a better chance"? But by the second or third generation the money is gone and the family has died out. It's striking how few old, well-to-do families we have in this country. So the best way to care for the family is to see that children grow up to be healthy, decent, independent individuals.

I often ponder the differences between the country (and of course the city) of my day and the present. Today's child is influenced by the radio and records, by newspapers and children's periodicals, by an unprecedented variety of illustrations; today people travel more and with greater ease. We knew nothing of the sort when we were children. I had nothing to read, no way of hearing or seeing new things. That's why the church was more important to us than it is to today's children. It was the only important building besides the castle, only we weren't allowed in the castle and we went to church regularly. So once a week we saw something huge, lofty, and ornate; we heard sermons and music; we gathered as a village. How different the sermons and the whole atmosphere would have to be today to attract the younger generation as it did seventy years ago. But here we are again up against the current religious crisis and the factors causing it.

SCHOOLDAYS

Apprenticeship

Mother saw to it I went to school so that, as she put it, I wouldn't have to drudge like them (my parents). One day I was praised by the church dean during his school inspection tour, and as a result I was allowed to go on with my studies. Mother was from Hustopeč, so I was sent to the *Realschule* or German technical school there. I lived with my aunt, and one of my cousins came to live with my family in exchange. I had never thought about what I wanted to be, though at one point, when a tailor was making some clothes for us at home, I liked what he did, and I liked what blacksmiths did, their trade being the one at which I had most often seen men working. Considering how religious I was, it's odd I never thought of becoming a priest. A boy in an out-of-the-way village has few living examples of anything beyond his circle of farmers and artisans: the teacher, the chaplain and dean, the owners of the estate and their servants, and a merchant perhaps. What a boy becomes is determined not so much by his gifts as by the opportunities closest at hand.

The *Realschule* in Hustopeč was run by the Piarist Brothers. I remember the rector, a stout, handsome man getting on in years, and Professor Vasatý, the brother of the Vasatý in the Young Czech Party and a good-looking young man who was proud of his order's habit with its black belt and had quite a following among the girls as well. I was very fond of him. He was the first Czech from Bohemia I got to know, and so I found him interesting. He would chat with me about all sorts of things. To this day I can picture the way he walked.

I did well at school. I was especially attracted to physics, that is, mechanics. I recall even now my astonishment at our professor's explanation of a wheelbarrow as a one-armed lever and wheel that followed the theoretical mechanical formulas. It opened an entirely new outlook on life for me. I always like to see theory being worked out in nature, society, and day-to-day work and to find the general laws behind them. That first time was a revelation.

After two years at the *Realschule* I was supposed to go on to the teachers training college, but I couldn't be admitted until I was sixteen, so there was the problem of what to do with me in the meantime. For a while I hung about doing nothing in particular. That was in Hodonín. My former masters advised my parents to have me taught a trade, so they sent me to Vienna and apprenticed me to a *Kunstschlosserei*, a specialty locksmith, because I could draw a bit. The foreman sat me at a machine that made taps for boots. You put in a little iron rod, pulled a lever, and out dropped a tap in the shape of a miniature horseshoe. I didn't mind it for a day or two, but for a week, two weeks, three weeks . . . At the end of the third week I ran away and went back home. I had always liked work, but that monotonous factory work, those one or two movements over and over, was more than I could stand. I might have held out were it not for the fact that one of my fellow apprentices stole all the books I had saved from the *Realschule*. After work I would grab them and read. I was so upset at losing them that I ran home to Čejč. I particularly missed the atlas: I had spent every evening roaming the world with it.

Back in Čejč my father apprenticed me to the blacksmith on the estate, our neighbor. How I enjoyed smithing! It calls for strength and speed and a minimum of words: you must strike while the iron is hot. At that time the caste system was still in operation. The foreman was on top. He was followed by his journeymen, according to their age or length of service. Journeymen had certain rights, but if an apprentice ventured to do something he had not yet earned the right to do — smoke, for instance, or take out girls — he would get a good box on the ear. In summer we often worked from three in the morning till ten or eleven at night, mending plowshares and shoeing horses. But it's fine work: a smith at his forge and anvil is a master over matter. Once, when I was a student, I astounded a blacksmith in a village on the way to Brno by forging a nail in one heating of the iron. I don't know whether the fingers of my right hand are crooked from working at the anvil, but many years later, during my visit to Yasnaya Polyana, Tolstoy looked at my hands and asked whether I had been a workman.

I might have remained in the smithy had it not been for a curious coincidence. One day in Čejč I was carrying some buckets of water from the well to the forge when a gentleman came along the road and stared at me attentively. I recognized him as Professor Ludvík, who had given me piano lessons in Hustopeč, but I didn't say a word to him: I was ashamed at being so blackened with smoke, and I could see from his expression that he had not expected to find me a blacksmith's apprentice. When I got home, my mother said, "Professor Ludvík has been here, and he's left word for you to go to his father, the rector at Čejkovice, and work as his assistant." And that is what happened. I was fourteen and couldn't start the teachers training college for two years, so in the meantime I helped out at the local school. I got no salary, of course, but the rector gave me piano lessons.

Anyway, I taught the boys and girls what I could. After a while I started playing the organ in church on weekdays and singing at funerals, as school teachers had to do in those days. When I recited the Latin at funeral services, Father Satora scolded me for my bad pronunciation. I also wanted to understand what I was saying. It was then that I had my first run-in with the Church authorities. I taught the children at school, as I had been taught at the *Realschule,* that the sun is stationary and the earth revolves around it. When the children repeated it at home, their mothers went to the dean to complain that I was tainting the children's minds, teaching them things contrary to the Holy Scriptures. But Father Satora somehow managed to smooth it over. The annual fair happened to be taking place a few days later, and the farmers got together and came to the school to see me. I was startled: things looked bad, though I didn't mean to give in. Then one of them stepped forward and said, "You're doing a fine job with our children, teacher. Don't pay any attention to our women. Just go on teaching." And one after another they dug into their pockets and placed a four-kreutzer coin or at least a kreutzer on the piano. You must recall that I too went to a Church school and that during the sixties the Church's influence in the countryside was still strong.

I loved to read. The Čejkovice Castle had some old books left behind by the Jesuits, books written in the seventeenth and eighteenth centuries, all of them polemics against the Protestants. One of them was rather well known. It was called *Vogel, friss oder stirb* (Bird, Eat or Die), and it was a brutal refutation of Luther. I devoured the books, and they made me such an ardent Catholic that I converted the wife of the blacksmith to whom I'd been apprenticed. She was a German Protestant — her husband had brought her all the way from Germany — and I talked and talked until I talked her into converting. Hers was the first mixed marriage I had known, and at the time of course I saw it in a strictly Catholic light.

The German books had Latin quotations I wanted to understand. That was a further reason for learning Latin. I started studying on my own, memorizing the words in an old dictionary from A all the way to Z. I had and still have a good memory for words, but I didn't make any headway with the grammar. Later Father Satora gave me regular lessons. On his advice I went to Strážnice to take the Gymnasium (classical secondary school) entrance examination, and that is how I entered the (German) Gymnasium in Brno in 1865.

In Brno

So there I was in Brno. . . By the time I was in the second year, I had to support myself: my parents could not provide me with a regular allowance, though my mother — God knows how — did manage to scrape a little something together for me. At first I lived at a shoemaker's on New Street. There were about six of us there. For two gulden a month I had bed, breakfast, and linen. You can imagine what the coffee was like, but at least it was warm. Anyway, I had to give private lessons. My first pupil was the son of a railway official, and that brought in two gulden a month and Sunday dinner — I could have eaten three at a sitting! Then I tutored a baker's daughter. The baker didn't pay me, but I could take as much bread as I wanted. Besides, they were very nice people and we became friends. Because I was at the top of my class, I was recommended as tutor to the family of Le Monnier, the Chief of Police, who was about the biggest man in Brno. Later I took my meals there daily, which meant I could support my brother too, though he was never good at his studies. We boys had a fine time of it together: in the evening after work we'd play all sorts of games, and in summer we'd go swimming at Zábrdovice and eat bread, cheese, and a pint of beer at the brewery for six kreutzers.

I liked Brno because I had access to books there. Of course at the German Gymnasium I read plenty of German and Catholic propaganda, but that didn't bother me; on the contrary, then as in Čejkovice I devoured Catholic apologetics. I can still remember some of the novels. One was called *Fabiola* and was by Wiseman. Fabiola was a beautiful Roman maiden who died a martyr's death. The second novel was also a translation from the English and was called, I believe, *Die Märtyrer von Tilbury* (The Martyrs of Tilbury). The martyrs in question were Catholics put to death during the English Reformation. The third book was *Glaubenskraft und Liebesglut* (The Power of Faith and the Fires of Love) by a certain Madame Polko. It was about a young Catholic missionary who goes to India, where a beautiful Hindu princess, Princess Damajanti or something, falls in love with him, but faith overcomes passion, and it too ends in a martyr's death. I enjoyed it all tremendously — the missionary fervor, the proselytizing, and especially the constancy with which the heroes stood up for the faith, their martyrdom. I was quite overwhelmed.

To be precise, what impressed me most about Catholicism in my youth was first, its vigorous transcendentalism; then, its universality, its international, worldwide scope; then, the energy of its propaganda and missionary zeal; then, its attempt to create a unified view of the world and of life; and finally, the organization and authority of the Church. As I grew older, of course, I came across anti-Catholic works exposing the Church's absolutism, exclusivity, and acts of violence; even the catechists at the Gymnasium drew our attention to anti-Church and anti-religious writers by entering into controversy with them. I reached maturity during the rise of liberalism and its battle with absolute authority, both ecclesiastical and political. I couldn't avoid pondering books like Renan's *Life of Jesus* and the like. . .

*

Our catechist at the Brno Gymnasium was Father Procházka, one of the Christian Socialists of the day. It was by going to his meetings and others that I learned about socialism. When I was in about the fifth year, I announced to Father Procházka that I could no longer go to confession. Father Procházka was fond of me. He was a good and truly religious man. He admonished me even with tears, but I would not give in. I disliked the formalism of it. The boys would boast of the clever confessions they had made. Besides, I was tormented by the common practice of having a sin absolved today and sinning again tomorrow. Confess your sins. Fine. Everyone needs to talk things through with a friend, a kind, understanding person. But then go and sin no more. I didn't like the comfort of it all. That was why I stopped taking confession. Of course, I was beginning to have doubts about certain other Church doctrines at the time.

It was also the time when I had my first clashes as a Czech. Czechs and Germans were together at school, and we naturally quarreled and fought over the comparative merits of our nations. We Czechs were older because we'd had to slog away at German for a year or two, and I was older because I'd put in time at the *Realschule* and as an apprentice. We usually beat the Germans in our scuffles, which were innocent and harmless. The Gymnasium was German, but in my days the deputy headmaster was a Czech, Kocourek by name, the author of a Latin dictionary. He was a good fellow at heart but the laughingstock of the boys. Kocourek eked out a living making dyes. His hair and whiskers were white, and he would wipe his hands on them and appear before us all blue, green, and red. He was our Czech teacher, and since Czech was an elective subject, pandemonium broke loose during his class. He would beg us to be quiet — at least quiet enough to keep our shouting from being heard throughout the school — and when all else failed he would offer to tell us a joke. Then we were as quiet as mice. The poor man knew only one joke and a naive one at that, and he would draw it out as best he could to keep us still for the longest possible interval. But as soon as he came to the punch line, we would make such an uproar that he would clutch his head and plead with us to stop. Well, boys will be boys. . .

Kocourek was eventually replaced by a red-headed Teuton, and with him a strict German regime began. We had a Greek and Latin teacher who in Kocourek's time still signed his name "Staněk" but then took to writing it "Staniek" to make it look German. That really got to me. Once when I was being examined by him, I scribbled "Staniek = Staněk" in the margins of my book. Well, he snatched the book out of my hands and gave me a really hard time of it.

In the fifth year we got a new professor for Greek and Latin. His name was Wendelin Förster and he later made quite a name for himself as a Romance philologist. He was the strictest Teuton of them all. He pronounced Greek as if it were German — "Tsoyss" for Zeus — and forced us to do the same. To get back at him I started pronouncing Latin as if it were Czech. You can imagine how he fumed. But I said to him, "You are German, Herr Professor; you pronounce Greek and Latin in the German way. I am Czech, and I pronounce them in the Czech way," and stuck to my guns even when the headmaster called me in *ad audiendum verbum*, that is, had me on the carpet. I was given low marks in conduct for my disobedience and defiance, and in the end received a *consilium abeundi*; in other words, I was expelled and had to leave Brno. More about that later. But fortunately Police Chief Le Monnier was transferred to Vienna at the time and took me with him. I was admitted to the sixth year there, but only after his intercession on my behalf and only on probation.

As a boy I had no concept of nationalism other than a feeling for my village, Čejkovice. The name of the neighboring parish was Podvorov (Below the Court Village), but we of course called it Potvorov (Monster Village), and the Podvorov boys sang a song that began:

Čejkovice tots
Poke in chamber pots.

Every Sunday we'd come to blows with the Podvorov gang over who would ring the church bells. There you have nationalism in a nutshell. In Brno I began to understand what it means to be a Czech. Before that, at home in Čejkovice, I'd felt only a primitive socialism. National consciousness crystallized in me with a knowledge of history, and my knowledge of history came from the novels of Herloš, which I avidly devoured.

Think how exciting our history is. Take the Přemyslide kings and their policy towards Germany: how well they understood our international situation. Or the Reformation, the Counter-Reformation, the National Revival: how extraordinarily dramatic the struggle was. Then look at the map and our position on it and think how we have held out! That in itself makes it all worthwhile. We must get a proper grasp of our history. I know of none greater.

We shall always be a tiny minority in the world, but when a small nation achieves something with its limited means, what it achieves has an immense, exceptional value, like the widow's mite. We are not inferior to any nation in the world, and in some respects we are superior. This is now being recognized even abroad. Being small does not matter; it even has its advantages: we can be closer, get on better, feel more at home with one another. It is a great thing when a small nation among great ones does not lag behind but plays its part in the betterment of humanity. We want as much to ring the bells of the world as the Podvorov boys wanted to ring our Čejkovice bells. The problem of small nations is that we must do more than others and do it better. And if anyone sets upon us with force, we must hold our ground. Holding your ground is everything.

*

Even if we had no Czech books, we had Czech songs. We Czechs at the Gymnasium would get together and sing as many folksongs as we knew, copying out any that were unfamiliar. I remember some to this day. While studying in Brno, I would walk home to Čejkovice with other boys from our parts, singing all the way. Once we stopped at a well-known inn, and one of us — a devil of an eighth-year student (he later became a priest) — started making up to the hostess, a young woman and pretty, though unusually serious. When he finally took her round the waist, she opened the door to the next room and without a word showed us her husband lying dead on a pallet of straw, a candle at his head. . .

Once I took a sack of my mother's doughnuts, twenty or so of them, to Brno as a kind of present. When I got to Customs at Brno, the officer stopped me and asked what I had there. "Doughnuts," I said, and he told me I had to pay duty on them. What was I to do? I had no money, and I couldn't bear the thought of parting with them. So we sat right down at the gate, my pals and I, and made short work of them. Even the stern customs officer had his share.

The Wars of the Fifties and Sixties

As a boy I of course was terribly interested in war: it was part of a boy's education in those days. During my childhood and youth there were several wars.

In 1859 a fellow came back to our village from the war in Italy with a frostbitten foot. I listened breathlessly to the tales of his vicissitudes. He had the politics of it all oddly skewed: he was clearly ignorant of whom he had been fighting and why.

Then in 1863 there was the Polish uprising against Russia. By that time I read the papers — when I could get hold of them — and was a fierce partisan of the Poles. Several Polish rebels, including the woman adjutant Pustowojtówna, were interned at Olomouc, and all sorts of legends about them were making the rounds. For some time thereafter I was on the lookout for novels and "penny dreadfuls" dealing with the uprising. I couldn't think of anything else. Later I gave lessons to a fellow student who had been born in Poland, and he told me a lot more about it. I even started learning Polish.

In 1864 there was the war in Schleswig-Holstein, and I sided fanatically with the Danes: though a small country, they had stood up to two large ones.

When the War of 1866 broke out, we Czechs at the Brno Gymnasium put our heads together, talked it through, and resolved to volunteer against the Prussians (which didn't exactly mean we were pro-Austrian). One of our schoolfellows, the oldest and strongest among us, was actually accepted on the spot. But then the schools were closed and I went home to Čejč. Soon the Prussians won a victory at Hradec Králové

61

and the Austrians began retreating across Moravia to Hungary. Terror reigned: the Prussians were rumored to kidnap young boys and make them fight as soldiers. With this in mind I went to see my oldest friend in nearby Terezova and urged him to come and enlist in the Austrian Army according to our compact. Frantík tried to persuade me to run away and hide instead. As I say, Austrian regiments were retreating in the direction of Hungary, and a column of foragers had marched into Čejč. The officer in charge asked me the way to Hodonín, and I offered to guide him, so Frantík and I set off with the soldiers. On the way I told the officer I was thinking of joining up. He tried to talk me out of it, saying I was young and underweight, there was no doctor to examine me, the war would soon be over, and so on. As we were entering Hodonín, a house by the road caught fire and caused a panic: people said the Prussians had done it, they had spies all over. From Hodonín the soldiers set off for Hungary. I accompanied them as far as Holíč: I knew the countryside well and felt at home everywhere.

Near Holíč a Prussian outpost caught up with us. The alarm was sounded, and part of the infantry and cavalry turned back to face the Prussians. The fields were all hayricks and hillocks; the Austrian commander sat on horseback behind one of the latter. Evening was coming on and it was growing dark. Frantík and I, together with a Jew and a Slovak from Holíč, ran over to the hill near the graveyard so as to have a view of the battle. We hid there behind the wall. Frantík was frightened and took cover in a freshly dug grave; the Jew followed suit. The Slovak and I peeped over the wall. We saw the infantry column advance and fire. The Slovak said they were Italians and would run away. Then the cavalry charged. We watched them hacking away at one another. All at once I saw a soldier riding straight at us. When he came close I saw that he was the officer who had taken me with him and that his face had been slashed from temple to chin. I called out to him, and he rode along the churchyard wall to the gate. The Slovak, who was a sensible fellow, said to me, "Run to the nearest hut, pull a sheet off the bed, and dip it into the well." So off I ran, and he and the Jew (Frantík stayed behind in the grave) led the officer after me. I took a sheet from the hut and soaked it in the well, but the wet sheet was heavier than I had expected, and I had to lean my knees against the edge of the well to drag it out. In the process I tore the skin below my knee on a nail, but failed to notice it in the heat of the moment. Only after we had bathed and bound the officer's wounds and slipped off his clothes — the Jew took them away — did I realize I was hurt. I had meant to run on, but found I couldn't. I managed to get a lift in one of the army carts, and was duly bandaged up at the field dressing station in Pressburg. After that I went with Frantík to Kopčany, where I had relatives. There I heard that the Jew had been taken prisoner by the Prussians — the officer's uniform had given him away — as had the officer himself. The Holič skirmish took place on about the fifteenth of July, on a Monday, I believe, but I can't guarantee the accuracy of the date and I've forgotten some of the details.

That same year, 1866, I had another adventure. I had been going to Hovorany to see Father Satora, who had been transferred there from Čejkovice. Once I stayed with him till dark: he had officiated at an especially grand funeral, and I had gone along. I was walking home with a funeral candle in my hand when I noticed a man hiding behind a poplar tree on the other side of the ditch. I was pretty frightened, but I kept going, and as I approached him the man jumped across the ditch and lunged at my throat. It was all so quick I don't know quite how it happened. I only remember that as he grabbed me by the throat I gave him a shove and one of his legs slipped into the ditch. Then I smacked him across the face with the candle and he stabbed me in the side with a knife or something, but I managed to pull myself together and shot home like an arrow. Not until I was indoors and in the light did I realize he had cut through my coat and shirt and made a long gash down my side. But it was nothing. He must have mistaken me for somebody he'd been waiting for.

Later, during my first years in Prague, I began a novel (it was to be a kind of *Dichtung und Wahrheit*, a semi-autobiographical work) and included the adventure as I remembered it, though touched up romantically (my hero was a soldier, and so on). As you know, I gave up the novel long ago — I burned what I had written — but even now I sometimes see it in my mind's eye when I lie awake at night.

*

If you must know, that wasn't my first attempt at a novel: I began my first novel while at the Gymnasium in Brno. I was earning my keep by then and supporting my brother, I was the oldest in my class, I had stood up to my teachers, and I had been in love. In short, I thought I had experience galore and decided to write the story of my life. When I had finished several chapters, I read them aloud to my schoolfellows just before a swim. Of course the boys were more interested in the river and got impatient, but I didn't stop till I'd read the whole thing through. Then one of them, a boy from Haná, said, "I've never heard anything so ridiculous in all my life!" I burned it.

I'd tried my hand at poetry even earlier, when I was in Hodonín for a time after those two years at the *Realschule*. I wrote love poems to a girl there — we had been in plays together — but they must have been terribly unpolished: I hadn't a clue about rhythm or form. The boys at the Gymnasium made fun of me when I read them. It was then that I first understood what a humanistic education means. I'd like to be able to see the poems I wrote then. In Brno I came across Sušil's *Poetics* and tried under its influence to compose verse in every possible style, including the Indian. Later I gave it all up, though literature has meant a lot to me all my life.

*

Why did I leave Brno? For love, actually. While I was in the fifth year at the Gymnasium, my landlady had visits from her sister-in-law, a girl about my age, and the two of us fell for each other. She was my first great love, and I was quite carried away by it. Naturally I wanted to marry her and as soon as possible. As I say, I was supporting myself at the time, I was the oldest and biggest in my class, I had had run-ins with several of my teachers; in other words, I pictured myself a mature and independent individual. It goes without saying that her parents did what they could to discourage her and we had to meet secretly — in the street and so on. When it came out at school, I was summoned by the head-master — the worst they could do — and given an offensive sermon about my love, as if I'd been guilty of some form of immorality. I felt so slighted I was quite beside myself, and when he sent for the school porter to take me away I grabbed the poker and shouted I would not stand such insults to myself or the girl I loved. That was why I got the *consilium abeundi* for insubordination. The only reason they took no further action was that the headmaster must have known he was in the wrong.

Such was my first love. Since then I have given a good deal of thought to the subject of love on the basis of my own experience, of what I have observed around me and, mainly, of literature, which is of course largely concerned with love. I have said a great deal about my own later involvement and my wife's influence, and now I will only repeat that love — strong love, true love, the love of a man and woman who are sexually pure — is, as it says in "The Song of Songs," as strong as death, no, stronger than death, because it both supports life and creates new lives. Literature thus rightly devotes so much attention to love, though therein lies the difference between literature and Literature.

Vienna

Vienna had a decisive influence on my spiritual development: I spent the best part of twelve years (1869-1882) there (one of those years, 1876-77, I was in Leipzig). Moravia looked to Vienna at the time, and Brno was practically a suburb. The first time I went was as a locksmith's apprentice, and once, during the holidays when I was a Gymnasium student, I walked the whole way. Both times I fled from the place it depressed me so. In my more mature years I grew accustomed to life in the city, especially as it supplied me with the means to gain an education and earn a living.

I entered the Academic Gymnasium in Vienna as a sixth-year student and completed the course of studies in 1872. I soon found the life at school distasteful: I was more experienced and relatively older than the other boys and had to support myself. During my early years in Brno I considered good marks in school work important, and for several semesters I was top in my class. But I soon said to myself it was enough to get through my school work creditably and better to devote time to languages, poetry, and art and to reading historians, philosophers, and the like. I have always been a voracious reader.

My interest in religion, politics, and nationality issues provided a strong incentive to reading. In Brno I had become familiar with the theory of Christian socialism thanks to Father Procházka. I was not only able but forced to deal with the problem of nationality owing to its presence at the Gymnasium, where students and professors were classified according to nationality, and its presence in Czech and Austro-German politics — insofar as I could follow it. In Vienna I got in touch with various Czech societies, especially the academic one. As a Gymnasium student I couldn't be a member, but I arranged with the board to register as a philosophy student, because the final two Gymnasium years were until recently called "philosophy classes" or "philosophy" for short. Soon, however, a member of the board who had ideas of his own about philosophy accused me of being ineligible for membership, and right he was. I had learned my lesson, namely, that a lie will out even when it is a *fraus pia*, a lie in a good cause.

As to my future, I thought very little about it. While attending the Gymnasium in Vienna, I wanted to be a diplomat and thought of going to the School of Oriental Studies. I even started studying conversational Arabic. Then I discovered that the School of Oriental Studies admitted only sons of the nobility, and dropped the idea. I think that when choosing diplomacy what I really had in mind was traveling to far-off countries. I have always enjoyed travel, even atlas travel. I love maps to this day. And I have always been interested in the statistics about conditions in different places. On my school-leaving exam the geography professor asked me a question about the statistics of nationality and religion in Hungary. I knew more about it than he did. He and the inspector were so impressed that they closed their eyes to my ignorance in areas that interested me less.

After completing my Gymnasium studies in 1872, I entered the University of Vienna. I had naturally been long interested in philosophy. I remember going to Professor Zimmermann (you know him, don't you? — the Herbartian aesthetician) and asking him how to make a professional study of philosophy. He suggested I should read the whole history of philosophy and then single out the philosopher who most appealed to me as a subject for detailed study.

Since I'd read the history of philosophy and the works of certain philosophers while still at the Gymnasium, I knew I had a predilection for Plato (I have remained a Platonist all my life) and therefore signed up for Latin and Greek, wanting to read my Plato and all the other Greek and Roman authors in the original. Professor Vahlen gave us four lectures a week for a whole semester on Catullus alone. I had read all Catullus in one sitting, and he went on and on about him: how many manuscripts there were, what variants could be found in his vocabulary, what a certain other scholar had written about him, and why that certain other scholar was a fool. During that time my brother Martin died — a cold he had caught in the army had developed into typhus — and the World's Fair opened. The impressions made by these events soured me on philology, though not on Greek and Roman authors.

Along with philosophy I studied the natural sciences (and anatomy). I was interested in the physiological psychology in vogue at the time. I never wanted to be a professor: I was not so much interested in teaching things to others as in learning them, coming to know them myself. As Aristotle puts it at the beginning of his *Metaphysics*: It is in the nature of man to seek knowledge. Acquiring knowledge, mastering new data is a great joy; indifference, lack of interest is worse than ignorance.

How does an interest in facts and more facts tally with my Platonism? Why, perfectly well, believe me. I want to know the facts, but I also want to know what they mean and where they lead. Which is metaphysics.

*

How did I support myself while at the University? I gave lessons. A Czech by the name of Bílek ran a school in Vienna, and he found me a tutoring job in the family of the director of the Anglo-Austrian Bank, Schlesinger. There I earned a hundred gulden a month plus full board, which was more than enough. In the circle of their family and friends I came to know how the rich live. They are not happy: their wealth is a wall cutting them off from others and often leads to follies and perversities.

Friendship is as strong a feeling for a young man as love. I had a dear friend whose name was Herbert and who studied at the Gymnasium with me. He was a gentle boy, a fine boy, and a devotee of geography and history. But he was always in bad health and died before the end of his Gymnasium days. His late father had been a doctor in the family of some Transylvanian duke or other. I used to go and stay with him and his mother and two sisters. I remember him well to this day and named my first son after him.

Other Viennese friends included my pupil Schlesinger, my Brno colleague Všetečka (later professor at Jičín), his friend Weigner (later director of the weaving school at Warnsdorf), and Šimon Hájek (later professor in Moravia), and in Leipzig I was friendly with the future lawyer Carl Goering. Literature created a certain bond among us, but in the main it was sheer camaraderie. We agreed to meet every ten years, I think, and talk over our lives. In fact, we've never had even a single formal meeting together, but we have kept in touch.

Herbert inherited a large library from his father, and the two of us read the eighteenth- and early-nineteenth-century German classics together. At the same time I wallowed in French literature: Chateaubriand, Musset, and the like. Hebbel was popular then among the young people in Vienna, but I have always been skeptical about fashionable trends. Wagnerian nationalism — that is, Wagner's music and the Germanic philosophy of both him and his commentators — was all the rage among the German students, but I can't say I liked even the music. Viktor Adler and Pernerstorfer, who later became Socialist members of Parliament, were also nationalists at the time. I had only minimal dealings with them then. When the second edition of Marx's *Capital* came out — in 1876, I believe — I plodded through it conscientiously, but even then I couldn't accept his Hegelian philosophy and materialist view of history. I studied the economist Menger very closely and went to his lectures, and later in Leipzig attended the lectures of the eclectic Roscher. On the whole I was rather isolated even in my interests.

Having been forced to work for my living from the age of fourteen, I had no time to fall into the bad habits of youth. I didn't even go through a puberty crisis. There is nothing evil about young love. I believe in the purity of youth. I feel the issue of young people and sex has been blown up artificially and unnaturally by literature, the theater, the press, and the like.

During my Vienna Gymnasium years I spent the holidays in Hustopeč. There I would visit the family of a Czech bandmaster who had a Czech girl staying with them. I found her interesting because she was the first Czech girl from Bohemia I had known. She was well educated and conscious of her nationality. I began to correspond with her, and once she happened to come to Vienna, where she stayed with her brother, an official there. He was a curious fellow: after borrowing money from me he seemed to want to offer me his sister in payment. I noticed he would invariably go out when I came to call, and he apparently arranged walks and excursions with the same intention. I was so repelled that although I knew she had no share in it I left off seeing them.

I recall another experience, one typical of youth perhaps. I once fell for a local girl I'd met at a dance in Klobouky, where I went for the holidays. It was love at first sight, and I wrote to her immediately, asking when we could marry. But no sooner had I sent off the letter than I realized I'd made a cruel and foolish mistake. Nothing came of it, of course.

If we brought up our children to have more boy-girl friendships, there would be fewer adolescent crises, unhappy loves, and disappointments. Just as parents should live in such a way as to set an example to their children, so society as a whole has a great responsibility to young people. When social relations are healthy, young people are healthy. And think of the ugly, slavish way society still treats women!

While we're on the subject, let me add that in my time many doctors claimed that sexual continence is unhealthy for a boy! Once I had a small rash on my face, and our family doctor advised me to go to a woman of ill repute because the rash was a sign of "exuberant blood." Parents had strange ideas about sexual matters too, though of course they were influenced by doctors. As a longtime private tutor I had to deal with the problem of self-abuse among boys. I first learned of the boyish vice at the *Realschule* and Gymnasium, and soon I had pupils who were addicted to it. I paid much attention to the problem and to sexual problems in general, especially later in life, when teaching ethics and studying literature and social relations. Experts say its harm to one's health is exaggerated, and that may be so. But as I see it, the moral harm is great: it leads to premature and immoderate sexual activity and especially, I feel, to perversion. I have learned much from the experience of our teachers, and they confirm my opinions. Sex education should come not only from the schools, however; it is primarily the obligation of the home. I recall a beautiful chapter in a novel by Mrs. Canfield where a mother explains the physical side of love to a daughter pained and distressed by the coarse advances of her betrothed. More tact and delicacy in our outlook on sexual matters and in our private lives — that is all we need.

Nowadays people are a bit more reasonable about such things. Sport has done a great deal of good. Athletes do not drink or smoke or indulge in debauchery: they want to keep fit. If it does not coarsen them in the process, sport will be a great advance and a return to the culture of the ancients, which is what Tyrš had in mind with his Sokol gymnastic movement. Sport also has the advantage of regulating or replacing innate or inculcated savagery. Nature, surroundings, and history encourage boys to worship war heroes and military rulers, while sport teaches them to overcome an opponent without blood and cruelty. It also instills a sense of honor in them. I myself had no opportunity to indulge in sport other than my participation in the Sokol movement, but even now not a day passes without my doing the Sokol drill.

On Schools

Our education of boys does not do enough to develop independence, self-reliance, and a sense of honor. My case was different: I was obliged to be independent as a child because I had to earn my keep, I had to look after myself and make decisions for myself far from home. Our educational system does not encourage pluck; it aims at material comfort, preferably in a government post that will provide security . . . I see the fear of death in all this, the fear of a life of initiative, responsibility, ambition. True, we lack a seacoast, we lack the consciousness of the world beyond; we sit like frogs in a pond croaking to one another. I'm always glad to hear of one of us going out into the world and getting somewhere, not as an emigrant — emigration is a form of flight — but as an enterprising Czech conquistador. Of course, poverty has much to do with it. Most of us are only one or two generations removed from humble origins as peasants, farmers, craftsmen. A boy coming from such a background does not do so much what he would like to do or be best at doing, as what is available, what will give him a safe income. Even cogitation is merely a superior kind of trade or perhaps even inferior to a good, solid trade.

I have observed that the best teachers — particularly in secondary schools — are good specialists. When teachers really love their subject, they make their pupils love it. Even though we forget nearly everything we learn at school, enthusiasm for learning, once aroused, never leaves us. Knowledge without enthusiasm is dead. Schools are not so much meant to teach great numbers of facts as to induce pupils to be precise, attentive, and systematic, teach them to observe life for themselves, and enable them to solve its problems, great or small, when- and wherever they arise.

What often happens instead is that teachers preach. In our country preaching occurs in schools, newspapers, and Parliament as well as in churches. I realize that educating the young is an extremely difficult proposition, but our secondary schools are too didactic: they teach rather than educate. Secondary school students come under influences that their teachers either do not suspect or else overlook. In England, for instance, a student receives much less general knowledge than here, but the English school forms character. Here young people must — temporarily, at least

— master a whole range of subjects, whether they find them interesting or not, but they will never learn to act effectively, mix with others, respond to life's vagaries. All too often our schools turn out green, doltish youths, and their cleverer, more energetic classmates reject school as boring, teachers as tyrants. Yes, even I used to have nightmares of going in for my exams again. School should not be a bitter experience, something to look back on as a nightmare. When school is a burden, the weak learn fear and the strong learn rebellion. And they both heave a sigh of relief once they've made it through the seven or eight years, those highly important seven or eight years when they are coming into their own physically and spiritually! That is slowly changing now. The old secondary school was too concerned with turning out future officials, that is, Austrian bureaucrats. Now it has and will have other duties. The point I wish to make is that if we feel the intelligentsia is in crisis we must get to the root of it, and that means the schools.

I was quite isolated growing up: in Brno I was older than my schoolfellows and thrown back upon myself; in Vienna I was not only a twenty-year-old among schoolfellows who were still children but a newcomer as well. Perhaps that is why I have always been critical, even mistrustful of fads, while our own young people race from one to the next, every five years a new generation rejecting what has gone before. True, we are a small nation, and having been cut off for centuries from the world of culture we are now trying to catch up: we grasp at every new idea, first from the East, then from the West, then from heaven knows where. But our cultural development has no head or tail to it. Looking around at what others have to offer is all well and good, but we must be sure to cast our nets wide and try more than the latest fad. We say we must open our windows to things foreign; well then, open them all, and the doors too! Of course, a small nation like ours, foiled and thwarted at every turn, must fall back on the culture of larger nations, but there are plenty of examples of small nations that have been culturally prominent and contributed a great deal to humanity. Historians and politicians are far too influenced by outside opinions of what constitutes a nation's worth. Hence the misunderstandings all over Europe, made up as it is of a number of small nations.

Another mistake we make is to underestimate who we are and what we have accomplished. Some people are always bemoaning the fact that America is larger than Czechoslovakia and Paris livelier than Prague. We are so intent on other countries that we overlook what we have at home. I realize we can't satisfy our hunger as readers by feeding only on Czech literature, but we must know it through and through to know what it has to offer. Anyone who complains about living on a small scale here is making a self-accusation: he himself is at fault. The man with a only veneer of education steers clear of the countryside and small towns: he claims he will be culturally buried there. In point of fact, it is a matter of comfort: he can be culturally alive only if he has his café and suchlike artificial stimulants. Think of Březina the poet: wisdom and culture are things of the spirit, not of chance surroundings. A lion is a lion even in a cage; a lion is never a donkey.

I am most aware of our lack of tradition when I look at our young people. True, we are far too prone to follow the beaten track (and do so more than we realize), but a beaten track is not tradition. Tradition is the common work of generations and requires great public discipline. We tend to start from scratch rather than build on the work of our predecessors. That is why we have so many small programs and associations with little influence on life and the way things evolve. True, we are a young nation and one continually renewed from below. The Counter-Reformation consciously wiped out the tradition of the Reformation — which made for a three-hundred-year gap — and today we don't know what to do with either the Counter-Reformation or the Reformation to say nothing of the period that preceded them. But I find the chief cause of our lack of tradition to be religious indifference: the average Czech intellectual has no use for the Czech past because it is so tied to religion. Instead he has his café circle or tavern table or the neighborhood or trade-union branch of his political party, and the stuffy atmosphere of any group of "regulars" represents the essence of small-scale existence.

Nowhere in the world do people grumble and grouse as they do here. It comes from our lack of pluck and from something even worse. To my mind what makes a person complain about politics, social conditions, the whole world is that he hates what he does for a living. The person who has no interest in his job, who does it only for the money, is an unhappy, frustrated person. I like to hear people talk with love and passion about their work. The things you can learn from them! Have you ever seen my sister-in-law Esperanza, a singing teacher, listening to a young singer? Have you noticed how her eyes light up? I love watching her throw herself into it. Parents and teachers should constantly be on the lookout for what their charges find exciting. We have enough practical schools — agricultural and technical — to enable everyone to choose according to his aptitude and inclination. There is no need in a democracy to turn each boy into a "gentleman" (which usually means an office penpusher). A farmer, craftsman, or workman is often far more of a "gentleman" than your average intellectual. The important thing is for each to find his place and be a complete individual. Each man and, yes, each woman.

THE YOUNG MAN

A Reader's World

Mrs. Browning says in *Aurora Leigh* that a poet can have two nationalities. I don't know about that. But it is often said that knowing a second language means living a second life. There I have a certain amount of experience.

I learned German as a child from my mother, though German was never a second mother tongue to me. Of that I became all too aware when I arrived at the German school in Hustopeč. The boys laughed at my German, and I had a hard time with written assignments. I did not get over it until I went to the Gymnasium, and even then not entirely. When my *Suicide* came out, a well-known German writer read it for style and found about a dozen Slavisms in the book. Even in German surroundings I spoke Czech almost exclusively: in my lodgings, with friends, in Czech associations. But I heard German at school and used it for tutoring; moreover, the bulk of my reading was in German.

I soon arrived at Goethe and Lessing. I was more attracted to Goethe's lyric poetry than to *Faust*, and through Lessing I discovered the Greeks and Romans. German opened up a great deal of technical literature and — in translation — world literature. I read Shakespeare and the other giants first in German.

The Viennese influence accounts for my interest in Austrian literature — Grillparzer and others — by which I tried to gain an understanding of the country. I paid particular attention to German writers from Bohemia (Hartmann and Meissner) and still follow them closely. Of those born in Hungary I was particularly engaged by the life and works of Nicolaus Lenau, and I came into indirect contact with Karl Beck in Vienna.

French I began while teaching in Čejkovice. Like several other nearby villages, Čejkovice was home to a number of descendants of French colonists, whom — if I'm not mistaken — Maria Theresa had resettled there from Lorraine. One heard names like Doné (Donné) and Biza (Bison) and stories about the colonists. Father Satora proposed that his junior teacher — Štancl — and I should study the language. He gave us some lessons (though he knew no French himself, he was good at grammar, and Latin helped), but they didn't last long. I took it up again in my third year at the Gymnasium: I wanted to compare French grammar with Latin. At the time I was tutoring a fellow student at his home, where a French girl was also giving lessons, and I tried hard to pick up the pronunciation. A good ear is supposed to help you pronounce a foreign language correctly. That would be a good thing for us Czechs and Slovaks, who are said to be so musical. I read as much French as I could lay my hands on. Out of the little savings I had, I bought French textbooks of history, geology, and so on. I read novels too — Balzac, Sand, Dumas *père* and *fils*, Hugo — but I was more interested in Renan. Père Hyacinthe was important then too. Not until I got to the University and later, when- and wherever I had access to libraries, did I begin to study the literature systematically. Then I read Rabelais, of course, who gave me a real feel for the French character, and Molière, whom I found highly attractive. My favorite poet was Musset, but I also liked Chateaubriand and even translated a few pieces of his: he was very close to my romanticism. The thinkers I found most interesting were Descartes and Comte. I was deeply moved by Pascal and studied de Maistre's Catholicism closely. I was equally taken with the Rousseau of *Héloïse* and the Rousseau of the *Social Contract*. I read Voltaire, though he made no special impression on me. D'Alembert did.

The French spirit is an admirable thing. The French are supposedly characterized by their "logic and clarity." Well, I'd call it "deduction and consistency." Plus the ability to take the initiative. The French Revolution and French socialism have given the world new problems and new solutions; French art and French literature are constantly coming up with new ideas. Then there is the French feeling for form, which makes them the true successors of the Romans and a living fount of classical culture.

Paradoxical as it may seem, the reason I never wanted to go to France was that I read French literature so much and so regularly. I don't think I was right, though: one can take in a nation with one's eyes as well. But I lacked the funds, and when at last I did go abroad I chose a country I didn't know so well from its literature. I still follow French literature, time permitting.

From the start I sought out French influences to counterbalance German ones. I was sorry so many of our people were only superficially enthusiastic about France or Russia (as when they sang, "Russia is with us, and whoever is against us, him the Frenchman will smite!") and in fact had no foreign language other than German. I took our Francophile and Russophile stance literally and tried to get a grasp of their language and spirit. And yet I am sometimes called a Germanophile! I, who more than most Czechs, was brought up on non-German literatures — in particular, as I say, French and Russian. Surely my book on Russia shows how much I read of the latter. (True, I have no sympathy with our great Slav enthusiasts who never bothered to learn the Russian alphabet.)

My favorite Russian authors were Pushkin, Gogol, and Goncharov. I consider Tolstoy a great artist, though I argued with him about his views. Dostoevsky held a sort of negative attraction for me: I could not accept the Russian and Slav anarchist strains in his work, which despite his return to Orthodoxy he never overcame. His duality made him the father of Russian jesuitry. I find something disturbing about Turgenev, but I like Goncharov and Gorky. I can read the other Slav languages tolerably well, but I prefer translations. I very much enjoy Mickiewicz and Krasiński.

I came to English and American literature later, chiefly under the influence of my wife. After many years of reading I know them quite well and currently read them more than others. I feel their novels at least are more interesting in both form and content than those of other literatures: they have more to tell me, offer me more subtle, insightful experience; I learn more from them.

Italian I can read and, if necessary, even speak, but most Italian authors I have read in translation (French, German, or English). The

Italian philosopher I find most congenial is Vico. Scandinavian literature and the literatures of other nations I know only in translation.

Yes, from childhood to the present I have been an insatiable reader. I have written an essay on my attitude to literature and may publish it some day. Among the issues I try to explain in it are how and to what extent a foreign people can influence us, by what means we acquire a foreign language and how far it enables us to enter into the spirit of its people, how much of that foreign spirit actually becomes part of us and how we process, digest, and synthesize it, and how our own character is intellectually and morally affected by our contact with it. For a long time now I have contemplated putting together the reactions to what I read in a sort of Reader's Diary. The books you go through when you start reading at the age of eight or ten!

From the start I read the great poets side by side with the philosophers and perhaps even more than them; after all, the greatest of them are known as "poet thinkers." I was no less interested in Goethe than in Kant, more interested actually. The same holds for other poets, starting with Shakespeare, though Dante, for some reason, has proved inaccessible to me. Poets and artists in general meditate on life and its problems no less than philosophers, and they are more concrete. They give an extraordinary wealth of knowledge to those who can read them; moreover, art is the surest way to come to know the soul and spirit of other peoples.

Unless I know the language of a country, I don't feel at home there. That is why I have deliberately traveled only to countries where I can speak to the people in their language. True, I've visited Egypt, Palestine, and Greece, but more for their ancient cultures than their current way of life.

I am consciously European in my culture, by which I mean that I find European and American culture (America is ethnically and culturally a part of Europe, transported — though not completely — to another continent) spiritually satisfying. I am quite unfamiliar with Eastern philosophy and literature, and what I do know I know at second hand because I have no oriental languages. The cultures of India, China, and Japan are inaccessible to me. I am rather skeptical of people who praise them to the skies and prefer them to European culture, though I realize they could claim I am like a blind man going on about colors.

As a European I am a Westerner, and I say so for the benefit of the Slavophiles, who see in Russia and Slavdom something better than Europe. The best Russians were Westerners too!

As for our literature, Czech and Slovak literature, I have read a great deal of it and feel I know it well, but you young people have grown up with it and can therefore make more out of it. As a child and a Gymnasium student I had less exposure to it than you. I came to it later, after reading widely in world literature, and because it couldn't stand the comparison I wasn't as enthusiastic about it as you can be. Most of my reviews of our writers are negative, but if you want to know whom I prefer, well then, Mácha* (though he represents only a beginning, a starting point), Němcová,* Neruda,* and Havlíček,* the latter as a poet as well as a journalist. I also found Vrchlický interesting — much of his lyric poetry is remarkable — but he was so prolific that he must be read selectively. I must have read all our Czech and Slovak novels, though I feel we are stronger in poetry. What we lack are novels dealing with our present-day national and political problems in such a way as to give both domestic and foreign readers an idea of our national character. Compare, say, the heights of the Scandinavian novel with ours. True, I enjoy certain passages in Čapek-Chod, Holeček, and Herrmann and I admire some of our young and even very young writers, poets particularly, but foreign literature affords me more food for thought and formal perfection. Ours teaches me about our national flaws and afflictions.

I feel a powerful artistic energy and a desire to enter the world arena coming from our young writers. Before and immediately after the war all our spiritual vitality went into politics; besides, we were in such straitened circumstances that a Czech writer could not live by his pen. Our independence and the Republic can liberate our spiritual life, and that will benefit, no, is benefitting our literature, as we can see from the interest both it and our art in general have aroused abroad.

All my life I have tried to enter into the literatures and thereby the cultures of our own and the Slav peoples and of Greece, Rome, Germany, France, England, America, Italy, Scandinavia, Spain, and — to a lesser extent — others. I have tried to make a fair and organic synthesis of them, and I feel I have brought them all into harmony with our national position. Still, the decisive, determining influence on me was not so much poets and philosophers as life itself, my own and the life of the nation.

At the University

The person who influenced me most as a teacher and a man during my student years in Vienna was the philosopher Franz Brentano. I frequently went to see him at his home, my obligations as a tutor preventing me from attending his (afternoon) lectures. Brentano had been a Catholic priest, but left the Church over disagreements with the Vatican Council and the doctrine of infallibility. I found the Council a stumbling block as well. But Brentano never spoke of religious issues either in his lectures or in conversation; he ceased doing so once he had left the Church. I derived a great deal from his emphasis on method and empiricism and perhaps most of all from the example of his penetrating criticism of philosophers and their teachings. Kant was his favorite target. Through Brentano I met the philosophers Stumpf and Marty. Meinong was also one of his students in Vienna at the time.

In Leipzig I met a number of other philosophers: Drobisch, Zöllner, Wundt, Heinz, Avenarius. I attended their lectures and came into personal contact with them at the Philosophical Society, where there was much lively discussion and where I myself lectured once on present-day suicide. Fechner was no longer teaching, but I visited him several times and liked him immensely as a person. I went to several lectures with Husserl, who later came under the influence of Brentano and his school. But at Leipzig I concentrated more on theology than philosophy, attending the lectures of Luthardt, Fricke, and others. Leipzig and its culture were particularly useful in helping me to understand Protestantism.

But the philosopher who influenced me most was Plato. First of all, for his interest in religion, ethics, and politics and his extraordinary combination of theory and practice. Then for that wonderful unity of world view, even if it derives from the fact that scientific disciplines were not well enough demarcated in his time. Another thing that attracted me to Plato was that he was a great poet and artist. As I have said, I have always loved poets and read them as much as philosophers, if not more.

Yes, to this day I am a Platonist. I can demonstrate it on the basis of my attitude to the theory of evolution. Don't worry. I promise not to speculate on Darwinism, neo-Darwinism, Lamarckism, vitalism, and so forth. I accept Plato's ideas in the following form: I believe in the idea of life, by which I mean that life is one but incarnate in a multitude of forms. Simply by being alive, each creature is like all others in certain respects and unlike all others in certain respects. By means of their similarities I can put together a scale of all the multitude of creatures from the simplest to man. We make just such a scale, just such a hierarchy, in all fields whenever we compare, organize, and evaluate. If you ask how the diverse forms and species originate, I respond that I do not know, but I refuse to accept Darwin's theory of mechanical chance, his principle of selection in the struggle for existence. For all his English empiricism Darwin uses a whimsical method: he turns a methodical scale based on likeness into an evolutionary scale of descendence. Natural scientists have opposed Darwin to Lamarck: neo-Lamarckism makes concessions to Darwinism; neo-Darwinism makes concessions to Lamarckism. Then there are the vitalists and their various schools. The lesson I draw from all this as a layman is that science tells us nothing as yet about the origin of the species, new species in particular. Darwinism is one of the forms of historicism and relativism against which I have always defended realism. I do not believe with Haeckel that the majority of creatures developed from a small number of original species or a single original species, nor do I believe, as I have said, in their chance, mechanical differentiation.

I adhere to the hypothesis of a Creator. Positing a Creator gives my ideas a certain metaphysical basis: ideas of Creation have always been with us. As you see, we can't do without a little metaphysics, but I hope I haven't overstepped the bounds I impose on myself in such matters.

From Plato I naturally came to Socrates, and it goes without saying that I compared him with Jesus, Jesus for me being the religious prophet,

Socrates the apostle of philosophy. How I loved his maieutic approach, his irony! Stopping a high priest in the street and questioning him about religion until the Greek cleric himself admitted to being a blockhead. Or talking to a general about war or a sophist about sophistry and demonstrating how each fails to think rationally about his own bailiwick. Think what times those were: an educator like Socrates, a philosopher like Plato, a scholastic and taxonomist like Aristotle! Think what Aristotle meant to the Middle Ages and to humanity! Aristotle has an odd relationship to Plato: he was Plato's pupil, he followed his teachings for twenty years, he was a Platonist, but he is more mature than Plato in that he tempered Plato's mythopoeic bent. Platonists and Aristotelians are actually two different types. I noticed this in my relations with Brentano, who was altogether the Aristotelian type.

When I was in Athens not long ago, what surprised me most was that there were neither steps nor even paths leading to the Acropolis temples. The Greeks placed their temples in the midst of nature, as if they had grown there of themselves, out of the soil. It was the Romans, those great formalists, who added steps to temples. Similarly, Greek philosophy, science, poetry, and art sprang up in the midst of nature and primitive life — a revelation, much as the Old and New Testaments are a revelation of the Palestine desert and primitive Judaism.

While we are on the subject of Greeks and Jews, think of the influence these two small nations have had on the whole of civilized humanity. The Greeks gave us art, philosophy, science, and politics, the Jews theology and religion. True, they were preceded by the Egyptians and the Babylonians, but their cultures were taken over and perfected by the Greeks. All Europe is still living off the legacy of the Greeks and the Jews. We scarcely notice it, but classical antiquity is everywhere. American civilization, however, clearly did not grow directly out of classical antiquity. It has a new element about it, the pioneer element, practical optimism. America has to learn from us, and we have to learn from America. But we still have the Middle Ages in us, and Catholicism, having absorbed much of the classical culture and adapted it to its own ends, is in a sense a continuation of antiquity. The Gospels have classical elements in them, after all. Consequently, Church writings should be included in the curricula of classical Gymnasia.

One thing the ancients lacked — and we in our northern climate possess — was a warm relationship to home, hearth, and family, to wife and children. The Greeks and the Romans did not know our winter; they did not know what it means to sit by the fire with children gathered round mother and grandmother. They talked politics and philosophy in the street; we shut ourselves up indoors and pore over books; Russians sit behind their stoves, musing more than thinking. The farther north you go, the greater the isolation and seclusion and the more important the family. Look around you. See the trees turning gold. Think of the variety the seasons bring and how much more complex and intensive they make farming for us. Italians know none of this; neither did the ancients.

*

It goes without saying that I am in favor of classical education, but it must be more than verbal gymnastics. Discovering the spirit of a nation is always a good thing. The ancients had relatively primitive religion, science, philosophy, and art as well as technology, economics, and politics; getting to the heart of things is easier with them, and their primitive nature is somehow congenial to the young. The fact that classical languages boast a certain clarity and logic means that Greek and Latin grammar teach accuracy and precision of thought and word. Then there is the grace, purity, and harmony of classical art: beauty of form and artistic perfection are eternal. Homer, Sophocles, and Aeschylus should be required — along with Euripides for the more mature and at least excerpts from Theocritus and others. Of the Romans: Virgil, Horace, Tibullus, Propertius, and obviously the historians. One or two speeches by Cicero are enough, his philosophical effusions being of interest chiefly to students of the Greek philosophers, who can judge how much he learned from them. Greek was to the Romans what Latin was in the Middle Ages and French became later. *Vox exemplaria graeca nocturna versate manu versate diurna!* (Study the Greek classics day and night!) Well do I remember that line. Like us the Romans had to deal with bilingualism. They were not ashamed to learn a foreign language. Nor did Greek hold back the Legions as they conquered the world. And if we're doing the ancients, let's be thorough about it. Why not include

Saint Augustine in the curriculum and a bit of Plotinus perhaps? In the original, I think, but with a good translation at hand. We have a few fine translations even now, but if I had the money I would start a fund for publishing standard translations of all the classics. How much could it cost anyway? And what a good deed it would be. After that I would publish translations of classics of other nations. And good biographies — we need them too. I would also found a sculpture gallery. And a model library, the living library of an educated person. I lie awake at night thinking about it. Heavens! The number of worthy cultural projects to be done! Some day we may even come up with a genuine cultural policy.

Other philosophers who influenced me? Comte, Hume, and Mill — greatly. Nor must we forget that we are affected by people and writers with whom we disagree.

*

Czech life in Vienna revolved around the workmen's associations, the Beseda patriotic society, and the students' Academic League. For nearly two semesters I was head of the League. Why? Well, someone had to be, and I had a little money, most of which I gave to the League when it needed it. I never dreamed of putting it into a bank.

One thing we did was to hold a celebration in honor of Alois Vojtěch Šembera — yes, the man who wrote the history of Czech literature. He taught Czech at the University of Vienna and was active in the Manuscripts Controversy.* He was so bitterly attacked for maintaining the Manuscripts were forgeries that his only son, a gifted man, consciously turned German. Besides that son, Šembera had a daughter, Zdenka, a good deal older than I. She was well educated and energetic, and the students considered her the model of an emancipated woman. She helped us to organize the Šembera celebration. I later corresponded with her, especially from Leipzig.

My contribution to the Šembera volume was an article on progress. At about the same time, I published another early work, an article on Plato's patriotism in a Moravian journal, using the pen name Vlastimil ("lover of one's homeland"). Later my chauvinistic opponents in Prague reproached me for having dropped the name when I started teaching at the German University there; in fact, I dropped it because I was ashamed to trumpet my patriotism in such a way. While a lecturer at the University of Vienna, I also published a Czech lecture on hypnotism, I wrote essays on activist politics for the *Moravská orlice* (Moravian Eagle), and I sent Vlček two articles — one on Schopenhauer, I don't remember what the other was about — for his *Osvĕta* (Enlightenment). When Vlček didn't publish them, I thought it was because my Czech was rough and bristling with Russisms: I was reading a lot of Russian literature at the time. Later, however, when I happened to be living at Vlček's, he told me he hadn't published the Schopenhauer piece because Tyrš was writing about him. In October 1875 I met Durdík at Brentano's and he told me Vlček hadn't accepted the piece because Tyrš and Zákrejs were planning to introduce Schopenhauer to the Czechs.

In 1876 I completed my doctoral thesis, *Plato on Immortality*, which in fact dealt with what Plato had to say about the soul. I later burned it along with many other manuscripts. It contained some good ideas, but why bother to keep it?

*

When I left for Leipzig in the autumn of 1876 I went as a doctor of philosophy. Leipzig will always be for me the place where I met my wife.

At the University there I attended lectures on philosophy and theology. I studied Protestantism and the form it took in a cultured Protestant society. If I remember correctly, I wrote the article on progress there in Leipzig. A scholar may want to use it to trace my development in matters of religion. At the time my ideas were not sufficiently clear or differentiated.

I kept up a correspondence with my friends in Vienna. There were a number of Czech philologists in Leipzig preparing for careers in Russia; there was also a Russian seminar and even, I believe, a Russian dormitory where all the students learned Russian while doing philology at the University. I was in touch with some of them.

I spent quite a bit of time at the Czech Club, whose members were mostly workmen. I did, however, meet a writer there, a Lusatian by the name of Pjech (spelled Pech in German) and an ardent lover of our

Havlíček. I had been interested in Havlíček since my schooldays in the mid-sixties. We would copy out his satires and anything else we could lay our hands on. Pjech told me in no uncertain terms that Czechs ought to study Havlíček more seriously than they had, and owing to a curious development I was later able to respond to his appeal.

I also became interested in observing the Lusatian Sorbs.* There were quite a few of them in Dresden, and from time to time I managed to chat with the group that gathered at the Catholic Hofkapelle. Using Pjech, the German translator of Pypin-Spasowicz, as my example, I watched how a Lusatian turns into a German and what Slav traits the Lusatians retain. After moving to Prague, I made a number of trips to Bautzen, their center, to continue my observations.

While in Leipzig, I studied spiritualism as well. I had read about various kinds of occultism previously, but in Leipzig I came into actual contact with spiritualists and was able to observe them at first hand. I believe the astronomer and philosopher Karl Friedrich Zöllner was sold on the idea, and I had undertaken a rather detailed study of hypnotism while still in Vienna. I need hardly say that I failed to be taken in by spiritualism and occult apparitions. There are certain phenomena we don't understand, but heavens! what *do* we understand?

Miss Garrigue

A fateful event took place in Leipzig in the summer of 1877, one that proved decisive for the rest of my life and spiritual development: my acquaintance with Charlotte Garrigue.

I had heard a lot about her and her family, especially her father's family, from the Goerings: Frau Goering kept the boarding house where I stayed in Leipzig. The Garrigues, I was told, were descended from an old Huguenot family. Mr. Garrigue, who was born in Copenhagen, had met the Goerings in a Leipzig bookshop. He later emigrated to America. His wife — Charlotte's mother, née Whiting — was from the American West and likewise of old lineage. A father descended from Huguenots and a mother from the pioneers who settled the West — what a tradition of vital, moral energy!

In 1870 Mr. Garrigue visited Germany with part of his family. Charlotte was already studying music seriously. She was a pianist and had visited Liszt and learned a great deal about him and his circle. She went to concerts at the Gewandhaus and heard motets at Saint Thomas', which upheld the tradition of Bach, its one-time choirmaster. Her closest friend was a Ukrainian woman by the name of Kirpotina. In 1877 Mr. Garrigue sent her back to the Goerings to study at the Conservatory, though a partial paralysis of the hand interfered with her musical career.

I was naturally curious about her in advance. When the time came for her to arrive, I waited by the window and watched her alight from the carriage. One day we all went for an excursion in the area outside Leipzig, with those Slav villages that made such an impression on Kollár* — you know which ones I mean, don't you? Well, the ferry that took us across the river rammed into the shore and Frau Goering fell in. The poor woman was terribly stout and would have drowned, so I jumped in after her and pulled her out. I caught a chill or something, and the doctor ordered me to spend a few days at home. Because I couldn't go to lectures, I suggested to Miss Garrigue and Fräulein Goering that we should do some reading together. We read English books, some poetry, and Buckle's *History of Civilisation in England*. That was when we got close.

When Charlotte went off to visit a friend in Elgersburg in Thuringia, I realized what I felt for her and wrote to her proposing marriage. Her answer was equivocal, so I plucked up my courage and went after her even though I could afford only a fourth-class seat. We came to an agreement on the spot.

Then Charlie went back to America and I to Vienna. I plunged into my work on *Suicide*, my *Habilitationsschrift*, the postdoctoral thesis required to qualify me for a post at the University. Suddenly I got a telegram from Mr. Garrigue saying that Charlotte had fallen from a carriage and been badly hurt and that I was to come at once. Just as I was about to leave, I had a letter from her saying it wasn't so bad as all that and I shouldn't interrupt my work. But I was worried and went anyway. It was 1878 and I took the *Herder* via Hamburg and Le Havre to America. In those days the voyage took twelve to fourteen days, but our passage was exceptionally stormy and took seventeen. Like many of the Hamburg-America Line ships, the *Herder* was abominable. She went down on her next voyage; the *Schiller* was lost in the same way. I was lying in my bunk one night when I heard an awful noise and turned to see water gushing into the cabin. I certainly thought we were going under, but whereas all the other passengers panicked and started rushing about, shrieking and praying, I lay quite still and waited to see how it would end. As it happened, it was just a cask of drinking water that had got smashed. When I arrived, I found Charlotte nearly well again.

But what now? I couldn't make up my mind whether to stay in America and find employment there, for by leaving I had lost the lessons that supported me in Vienna. I thought I might find a university post somewhere or work on a newspaper. In the end, however, we decided I should go back and finish my thesis. I asked Mr. Garrigue to give us the money to live on for three years until I could support a family. Old-style Viking and American that he was, he assumed that a man doesn't marry until he can support his wife on his own. At first he refused all support, considering it a form of dowry, but then he gave us three thousand marks and our passage back to Vienna. In addition, for some time thereafter he sent us an occasional small sum. Our wedding took place on the fifteenth of March, the civil ceremony at City Hall in the morning, the religious ceremony that evening at home in the family circle. A week later we were on our way to Vienna. It was on that journey that I had my second look at Prague.

*

As I believe I've mentioned before, Charlotte's family was Danish on her father's side and American on her mother's. Both families traced their genealogy back a long way. The Garrigues originally came from the south of France — there is a mountain range there still called La Garrigue — and are said to be descended from the Capets and even Louis IX, Saint Louis; the Whitings are an old, I might almost say aristocratic, family going back to the Pilgrim Fathers who left England in the seventeenth century on account of their religious convictions. It is worth a great deal to know your ancestors stood for something and were decent people. Tolstoy once told me with great enthusiasm about what fine people certain of his forefathers were. Having tradition and a shining example in one's background is a great stroke of fortune. On the spear side, that is, on the paternal side my children have Slovak peasant blood, and having decent peasant or workman forebears is no worse. But it is good that Charlie had by tradition assimilated a combination of gracious everyday manners and a need for freedom and honesty. My friend Hanuš Schwaiger, the painter, who regularly associated with aristocratic families, often said of my wife that in her bearing, in her every movement, she was the greatest aristocrat he had even seen. Yet when in 1905 a band of workmen demonstrated for free and equal suffrage and the secret ballot, she marched in their midst.

Charlie was one of eleven children. Two were boys: one was in business; the other, elder boy had gone to college but died young. The girls were highly gifted and independent: two of them are still excellent music teachers. Each family member was of a different faith, having been brought up in religious freedom and encouraged to make a personal commitment. Mr. Garrigue was an agnostic — in those days agnostics were often called atheists — but extremely moral, a good husband and father and a real American, a man who reared his children to work hard and respect the truth. Charlotte was a Unitarian.

She was beautiful to look at. She had a magnificent intellect, better than mine. That she loved mathematics is telling: all her life she longed for precise knowledge. Yet she did not want for feeling. She was deeply religious. So unshakable was her belief in immortality that she regarded death as the passage from one chamber to another. Lacking all trace of the moral anarchism so widespread in Europe, on the continent, she was clear and firm on political and social issues. She was absolutely uncompromising and never lied, two qualities that had a great influence on my development. She gave me the best that Protestantism has to offer: the unity of religion and life, that is, religious practicality, religion for every day. I came to know the depth of her convictions in the debates we had in Leipzig. Her poets were mine — Shakespeare and Goethe — but she saw more deeply into them and used Shakespeare to correct Goethe. We did everything together; we even read Plato together; our whole married life was a matter of cooperation. She was extremely musical. She loved Smetana and wrote an analysis of his second quartet for my journal *Naše doba* (Our Times), claiming it revealed his mental disorder. She did more work on Smetana; perhaps it will some day be published.

I could tell you much more! Our union was so strong. . . When she fell ill during the war, I had a premonition of it, far away as I was. And when I came home in 1918, all I could think of amidst all the glory was taking care of my patient.

She was American, but she became morally and politically Czech; she believed in the genius of our nation and helped me in my political battles and all my political activity. I was forced to work without her when the war came and I went abroad, but I always knew I was acting in harmony with her. There were times when, far as we were from each other, I could actually feel our thoughts coming together. It wasn't telepathy; it was the parallel minds and feelings of people in complete harmony and with identical ways of looking at the world. A woman, she believed, does not live only for her husband nor a man for his wife; they must seek and fulfill the laws of God.

On the Threshold

Yes, my marriage completed my education, my *Lehr- und Wanderjahre*, as I might put it, with Goethe. I was twenty-eight. Until 1882 I lectured at the University of Vienna.

I was constantly anxious about making ends meet, yet bankers came to offer me their services for the American millions I had married. While we were in Klobouky for the holidays, a district-wide delegation asked me to build a railway line from Hustopeč to Klobouky. Oh, the irony of fate, though it was not without its humorous side: one Klobouky burgher paid us a call and hemmed and hawed until we finally got him to admit that the reason he'd come to have a look at my wife was that he'd never yet seen — a Negress!

The difficulty of making ends meet increased when during my second holidays I caught typhoid fever and returned to Vienna late. Luckily I got lessons thanks to Frau Hartmann, the widow of the revolutionary German writer Moritz Hartmann. I also lectured to a ladies' club at the house of a famous surgeon by the name of Billroth. My first lectures at the University were on pessimism. During those years as a lecturer I felt the spiritual need to deepen my knowledge. My range was broad, but I lacked depth and system. As I've said, I studied the literatures of the principal European nations and attempted a philosophical synthesis in both theoretical and practical terms.

Meanwhile, thanks to the efforts of our members of Parliament, the Czech University was founded in Prague, and in 1882 I was appointed professor of philosophy there. I would actually have preferred a chair in sociology, but Austria had no such chair at the time. Sociology was recognized as a science in France, England, America, Italy, and elsewhere, but in Germany and Austria learned circles refused to hear of it. In Germany there was a field called philosophy of history, but its relationship to sociology and history was unclear. Even my thesis on suicide, which had qualified me for university teaching, belonged, as it were, to no field: one professor of philosophy thought I should send it to the Faculty of Law, another thought it had something socialistic about it. I owe it to Brentano and Zimmermann that it was accepted as a *Habilitationsschrift*.

Methodologically speaking, my work on suicide belongs to the philosophy of history, that is, to sociology, but its subject matter is our great period of transition. Some critics at the time pointed out that I had introduced a new field into the study of philosophy and applauded me for taking up the burning issues of the day and of life in general.

At the same time it illustrates my nature as a scholar: synthesis side by side with analysis. Yet for all that, my opponents in Prague long pronounced me an absolutely analytical, critical, and skeptical spirit. I myself didn't think of playing the role of critic at first. Until I left Vienna, I wrote nothing in a critical, polemical vein, though I had been invited to contribute to various journals. I was preparing my lectures and working out my ideas, which I planned to set forth in a series of theoretical works. Though who knows? Nature will out. Perhaps I'd have turned to practical affairs even if I'd remained abroad. But when I came to Prague and saw the dearth of critical studies, I set about righting the situation in my journal, *Athenaeum*, using it as a kind of conduit for ideas. Perhaps I was a bit nervous and impatient and I really didn't want to go to Prague. But *nolentem fata trahunt*, fate drags the unwilling, and from then on matters developed of their own accord, independent of my will. I have been drawn into all my battles kicking and screaming, making mistakes through ignorance of the situation. Even after I'd entered politics, I had no desire to found a new party. It was circumstances that got me into it all. To this day I very much dislike appearing in public and do so only when I must. Of course, once I set myself a task I will not shirk it; what I start I finish.

I am simply giving you the bald facts, but the move from Vienna to Prague represented a fresh crisis for me, one I experienced while still in Vienna. I feared the smallness of Prague. I was a stranger to its people and to the life of the nation though I'd made occasional modest appearances as a Czech writer. My feeling of alienation in Prague only increased during the battle over the Manuscripts and the political activity that followed. By basing my concept of nationality and statehood on morality, I clashed not only with political parties but also with a narrower circle of notables who placed nationalism above everything and regarded it as the *vis motrix*, the moving force behind all private and public life. Today I realize that the reason I made mistakes — mistakes in both theory and practice — was that I was not clear enough about my position. But more about that some other time.

What? It's nearly ten? Time for my daily report. You know, I haven't stopped working since the time I was a blacksmith's apprentice in Čejč. When I became president, the German philosopher Friz Mauthner paid me a visit, saying he merely wanted to see how a happy man looks. Happy? Well, yes. The main thing is to have a life rich in events and inner development, and in that respect I can be satisfied.

Book Two

LIFE AND WORK

NEW PROJECTS

Privatdozent

Life as a married *Privatdozent*, a non-salaried lecturer, in Vienna was not easy, but it was rewarding. We lived in a single room with one window and an entrance hall, which by an odd coincidence was just next door to the place where I had worked as a locksmith's apprentice in my youth. We made our breakfast at home, but took the other meals in a cheap tavern around the corner. Yes, we lived like students, but it was fine. Things were harder when the children came.

I was reworking my *Suicide* thesis at the time. I had submitted it before leaving for America, but it had not been accepted. I knew what needed to be done, but lacked the courage to say plainly what I had in mind. Professor Brentano advised me to revise it, so I set to work. Then my wife took an interest in it, and it became our first cooperative effort. The new version secured my appointment at the University. It was actually philosophy of history, of the contemporary period, mainly. I would formulate it more precisely and amply today, but I would make no substantial changes.

Since a *Privatdozent* does not receive a salary, I earned my living by tutoring. For a short while I also worked as a temporary teacher at a Gymnasium, but teaching at the secondary-school level was not for me. I tutored the son of Professor Theodor Gomperz, the philosopher and classical philologist. That boy, Harry Gomperz, is now professor of philosophy in Vienna. I coached him in Latin as well and came up with my own special approach: I would have him translate sentences about things that interested him in daily life; or when he had to learn, say, the multiplication tables, I would have him learn them in Latin. It proved highly successful. At one point I lectured on philosophy to a ladies' club at the home of Billroth the surgeon and to another club of the same sort at the house of Frau Hartmann, the widow of the German poet from

Prague. The income that came from all this was small and tenuous, and I must say I occasionally found myself in the most straitened of circumstances. The worst thing about it was being forced to borrow money. Once I even borrowed eighty gulden from Brentano, which I didn't pay back until after I got to Prague. Yes, it was awful to have to go and borrow, but I'd made up my mind that my wife should want for nothing, and that helped me go through with it. Once when things were bad, I had a visit from a young man, Herr Oelzelt-Newin, later lecturer in philosophy at the University. At that time he was just entering the field and asked me if I would read the philosophers with him, Kant in particular. He paid me well. By that time we had two children, Alice and Herbert; I had just got over my typhoid fever, and Charlotte had just fallen ill. And then Herr Oelzelt-Newin lent me several thousand gulden. Good lord, what a fortune it seemed! He too had to wait until Prague. These difficulties lasted three years, from 1879 to 1882, but you can stand a great deal if you've got a taste for work and a sense of duty to your family. This was how I spent my time: in the morning I prepared my lectures and looked up references in the library; twice a week I lectured; in the afternoon I gave private lessons, and in the evening I got *Suicide* ready for the press. For social life I had neither the time nor the inclination. We spent our holidays in Klobouky, near Brno, with my parents, where, as I've said, people came to look at my Negro wife and ask me to build them a railway line with my wife's millions.

*

I knew that there was no chance of my being appointed professor at the University of Vienna for a long time to come and that I'd have to go either to the university at Czernowitz or to Germany. But it was clear to me that if I went to Germany I'd become a German writer and have to publish in German, while remaining a Czech, though a lost Czech, like our tailors in Berlin and farmers in Texas. You are what you're born. Then the Czech University was established in Prague, and I was invited to go there. Well, I went.

*

97

Willingly? More like the opposite. I was apprehensive on account of my Czech and shrank from the conditions prevailing there in literature and philosophy. What's more, I did not know Prague at all; I had only passed through. The first time — fetching my pupil Schlesinger from Mariánské Lázně — I spent the evening at the Arena Theater and saw a stupid farce; after the theater I went to a café and observed the strange business of prostitution. A bad impression, in other words. The second time I was on my way back from America with my wife and we only spent the night there. Besides, my knowledge of Czech literature was quite unsystematic. There had been almost no Czech books available at the Gymnasium in Brno, and in Vienna I simply read whatever came my way. In Brno I would buy the Kobr Library editions of Rubeš, Klicpera, and other graybeards of that ilk and compare them with Goethe and Lessing! In Vienna I read Vrchlický and other poets, but Mácha was my favorite. The Academic League held an occasional literary gathering, but that was not enough. My association with Professor Šembera's family and especially with his daughter Zdenka provided greater literary stimulation. Most of the Czechs in Vienna were workmen, but I lacked the time to mix with them regularly. There were a number of Czech officials in the various ministries, but they formed a privileged circle to which I had no entrée as a student and for which I had no leisure as a junior lecturer. I therefore arrived in Prague knowing not a soul and quite ignorant of Czech life. Yet I managed to read my way into Czech literature and history and gradually even to penetrate into Czech society. My wife learned Czech and was convinced of our nation's mission. She proved a great moral support, especially as I soon found myself opposing public opinion.

My wife did not care for Vienna; I was accustomed to it: I had lived there for twelve years. In the families where I gave lessons I came to know a cultured, liberal Vienna, but I never became one with the city. Something about the Viennese spirit rankled, I suppose. The representative of "cultured Vienna" I felt and stayed closest to was the philosopher Franz Brentano. He was a great man and had a mind as keen as a razor. Although he did not write much, he had a considerable influence on his students (Carl Stumpf, Anton Marty, Oskar Kraus, but also Meionong, Husserl, and others). I loved his precise critical faculty and his anti-

Herbartianism, which was practically official aesthetic doctrine in Austria at the time. Besides, I had gone through the same conflict with Catholicism over the dogma of infallibility. As I've said, however, Brentano did not deal with religious issues in his lectures; he merely set forth the arguments in favor of theism. He promised to give proofs of immortality in his work on psychology, but in his lectures — as far as I know — he never said any more on the subject. I was interested in religion in all its breadth, so I traveled quite another road.

But the chief event in my life at the time was my break with the Catholic Church.

My *Suicide* shows how important I consider religion and particularly the loss of faith. I say there that a life without faith loses all its power and conviction, and I need say no more. I could go into greater detail about it today, but would essentially add nothing. That is how it is. And if it was not a finished product, well, neither am I. Did you know I was denounced as an atheist for it? In Leipzig I gave a talk on suicide at the Philosophical Society, and next day a young man came to me and told me trembling with excitement that for years he had been possessed by the idea of taking his own life and that my lecture had freed him of it. And the clerical and liberal parties accused me of advocating suicide! I was horrified then that people could be so evil-minded. I'm less surprised today. One German Catholic writer, Georg Ratzinger, realized at once that I had written a work on the philosophy of history and not an attack on religion, but our Czech Catholicism had not reached that stage of philosophical or theological development. More often than not, I had to deal with people who had no idea what I was talking about. If people could understand one another, we'd have democracy overnight. Without mutual understanding, without tolerance, there is no freedom. Only when people are completely truthful and open with one another can they really come to know one another, but without love there is no truth and without truth and love people cannot come together.

Moreover, only from such a base can a true marriage grow, a marriage pure and strong, the greatest gift of life.

*

How can people ask, I wonder, whether woman is man's equal? How can the mother who bears a child not be equal to the father? And if a man truly loves, how can he love someone beneath him? I see no difference between the endowments of men and women. When the late Professor Albert tried to convince me that women should not study medicine because they lacked the muscle and nerve for it, I said to him, "But they're not too weak to be nurses, are they? A nurse must tend her patients day and night; she must lift them, do everything for them. She needs more strength for that than you sawbones who operate no more than an hour at a time." That took care of him.

Let me tell you something: the issue of the equality of women is actually a middle-class intellectual issue. A farmer's wife or a laborer's wife often does the same work as her husband or at least works as much and as hard as he does. But when a man sits in an office, he doesn't think of all the things his wife is involved in: looking after the children, shopping, cooking, cleaning, sewing — doing any number of chores. Which of them works harder, I wonder? As for office work, the arts, the sciences, and politics, where women have only just begun to make their way, it is unreasonable to judge at this early date whether or not they are suited for them. Men have had thousands of years to master them and still often do them badly. The aristocracy have never worried their heads over the equality of women: women have reigned as queens and run countries as a matter of course.

A society that underestimates women is a polygamous society, and in fact we still live in polygamy. Primitive man did not take care of his children; he treated his wife like a slave or a beast of burden. But he was a hunter and a warrior who laid his life on the line for his family. As civilized as we are today, we have retained a gross form of polygamy: prostitution. And think of our dual sexual morality for men and women; think how it debases matrimony. The result, from my observations in life and literature, is that most unsuccessful marriages can be blamed on the man. Or if the woman is to blame, then the man is at fault as well: after all, men can still make what they please of their women. Not that women are all geniuses and angels; no, they are largely at the same stage of development as men. But they have one advantage: they live and carry out their responsibilities in such a way as to maintain greater purity than men; they don't drink or smoke so much, and they don't indulge in debauchery, which is why many a man seeks shelter in marriage.

I see only one way out, and that is education for monogamy. It is an all-encompassing task — cultural and to some extent economic and social. We cannot combat prostitution without eradicating the degrading poverty, the *paupertas meretrix* that goes with it. If we want to raise the level of morality, we must see to it that people can lead beautiful, pure, healthy lives, that mothers can give their children the care they need, that everyone can earn a living by honest labor. Then there is the problem of alcoholism, a problem that goes hand in hand with prostitution and poverty in general. I believe that a healthy, well-educated man and a healthy, well-educated woman will not have the complex sex problems of contemporary society. Their relation will be strong, healthy, and beautiful. A strong and healthy nature is a moral one or, rather, it is never base. So I am for the hygiene of life, spiritual and physical. I would not give young people many moral lectures. I would simply say, The wellspring of life can be found only by those who retain their youthful sense of purity. That and take more interest in your children. Fathers these days don't know how to treat their children; they pay very little attention to them. Believe me, our children suffer more from this than from anything else.

But the greatest argument for monogamy is love. True love — love without reservation, the love of one whole being for another — does not pass with the passing years or even death. One man and one woman for life, fidelity till death — that is how I see it. Happy is the man or woman who has lived a rigorously monogamous life. Yes, I am for divorce; I am for divorce because I want marriage to be love and not commerce or convention, not a senseless or thoughtless union. Though of course divorce can be abused like everything else. Love is great moral strength, the source of all mutual sympathy, help, and collaboration. A moral life presumes active participation in God's world order. Love, sympathy, synergy — such is the law of life whether it be for the couple, the family, the nation, the state, or humanity. I know no other.

Prague

Here is how I moved to Prague in 1882. A hypnotist by the name of Hansen was giving performances in Vienna, and I went to one of them and even visited him. Then some Czech students asked me if I would lecture to them on the subject at the Czech Academic League. In those days hypnotism was still looked upon as something mysterious, all "magnetism" and the like. I explained Hansen's experiments psychologically, that is, as hypnotism, lacking the technical knowledge to explain the stiffness of the body during hypnosis. After the lecture a Mr. PeNížek, a student of mine and later a journalist, advised me to publish it. He himself helped me to touch up my shoddy Czech and sent the manuscript to Prague. It eventually wound up in the hands of Professors Goll and Hostinský, who happened to be editing a book of lectures. They then published it and told Professor Kvíčala about me. Kvíčala was a member of Parliament and had been very active in the founding of the Czech University in Prague. The outcome of it all was that I received an offer to go Prague as an *extraordinarius* — that is, an adjunct professor — of philosophy with a promise from Kvíčala and the Ministry in Vienna that in three years I would be made full professor, an *ordinarius*. So I went. I found a flat in Karlova Street in Smíchov. It had a view of the Kinský Gardens but no sun, so I soon moved to Vinohrady and eventually to Vlček's house, Enlightenment.

An *extraordinarius* had a salary of eighteen hundred gulden. I probably could have earned a bit extra by taking on outside employment, but I preferred to be independent. We managed somehow, though I had to borrow money at times, which is always unpleasant. Three years later I was supposed to be made *ordinarius*, and the proposal for the appointment was already drafted when I got entangled in the Manuscripts Controversy. Some of the professors were against me and for the Manuscripts, and when my appointment came to a vote there were eleven yeas and eleven nays. It was for the Ministry in Vienna to decide, but with the wisdom of Solomon they left it unsettled: they didn't love me either, and they wanted peace at the University. Would you believe that people in Prague lodged denunciations of me in Vienna, saying I corrupted the young, I was a chauvinist, I repudiated Kant and German philosophy, and heaven knows what else? Archbishop Schönborn and several influential Czechs were against me. Hlávka, the founder of the Czech Academy, sent a transcript of my practical philosophy lecture to Vienna as proof that I had spoken about prostitution and was therefore corrupting the young. Can you imagine a situation in which speaking to law and philosophy students about a terrible moral problem like prostitution is forbidden? When I went to Russia, I was denounced in Vienna as a Russophile and Pan-Slavist. That was what I had to go through. Well, I'm over it now. It made me see how lack of freedom distorts the human psyche. Of course they mistrusted me in Vienna. That is why I had to wait thirteen years before I was made *ordinarius*. By that time Professor Hartl was Minister of Education, and he was sensible enough to stand up to all the complaints and denunciations.

So at first we had piles of worries. Then in 1884 or so the following incident took place. In Vienna I'd had a student named Flesch whose father was a prominent Brno manufacturer. He followed me to Prague and continued attending my lectures. A melancholy youth he was. By and by he went to Berlin, and there he shot himself. He left me some money in his will. After coming to an agreement with his father, I received a legacy of about sixty thousand gulden. That kept me above water. I was able to pay off my debts, help my parents, set up my brother Ludvík in a printing press in Hustopeč, and publish the *Athenaeum*. The money didn't last long. By the way, people said I'd inherited money from a suicide because I defended suicide.

I have a strange experience with money: just as things are at their worst it turns up from somewhere. I've never worried about going hungry; I've always believed that when you pursue a worthy goal you will not be left in the lurch. As Jesus says, "Seek ye first the kingdom of God, and all other things shall be added unto you." I am not fond of money: it has never been an end for me, only a means, whether my object was to help my neighbor or further a cultural institution. Perhaps what I like most about my position today is that I don't have to carry any money about with me. I have nothing in my pocket but a pencil. I don't even know what our money looks like.

*

I knew no one when I arrived in Prague, nor have I ever had many friends — I'm not good at opening up — so I associated mainly with my professor colleagues: Gebauer, Goll, Hostinský, Randa, and Ott. I liked Gebauer best. He was very impressive, and he taught me to be methodical. When he took notes, for instance, he would jot down each idea on a separate slip of paper and then file the slips where they belonged. He was on the staff of the *Národní listy* (National News) and taught me this about journalism: writing something once in a newspaper is not enough; you must write it over and over. A journalist mustn't simply say that such and such has been written and said; he must say it again, because the readership does not remember what it reads.

I also remember a group of Sunday hikers that included the Sokol leader Kröschel, Professor Kaizl and his uncle, Professor Heyrovský, the lawyers Marek and Brauner, and maybe one or two others. Every week we took long walks into the countryside, and in winter we had snowball fights. All my life I have kept up sports and exercises.

The one truly intimate friend I had in Prague was the painter Hanuš Schwaiger, a fine, tremendously fine fellow, with a wonderful, God-given sense of humor that never hurt anyone and that carried him through life and its hardships and kept him from souring. He and I and his friends — the painter Pirner and Professor Klein, the archeologist from Prague's German University — occasionally went out of an evening for a glass of beer or wine. Later, when I started turning against alcohol, poor old Schwaiger wrote to me — he was very ill by then — that I was right and had converted him and he would drink no more — "because I can't keep it down."

I had even more contact with Vojta Náprstek. Interest in America brought us together. I would go to the U Halánků reading room he had founded, and I once lectured there on poetry to a ladies' club. I later expanded the lecture into a small book entitled *On the Study of Poetry*. America was also a link between me and the poet Josef Sládek: he had spent time in America; I was married to an American. I once met the novelist Julius Zeyer at the Unionec or at the Náprsteks'; he struck me as rather effeminate. I would see Neruda every once in a while when his servant took him out for a walk; he was ill by then. I was interested in him and held him in great regard, but never actually got to meet him — perhaps because I'd heard he was on Grégr's side in the Manuscripts Controversy, though that may not have been true. I went and had a look at Bedřich Smetana at his table in the Café Slávia a few times before he died. I knew Svatopluk Čech slightly and wrote an article for his journal *Květy* (Blossoms). He was a shy, reticent creature; even in his poetry I could feel an inability to face facts and look life straight in the eye. Take the satire in his *Songs of a Slave*: it is absolutely impersonal, general, vague.

As for the University, well, at first the most important person was of course Kvíčala, then Tomek. I was closer to the younger men like Gebauer, Goll, and Hostinský. Many of the chairs had yet to be filled, but a kind of social aristocracy had formed among the offspring of the great national revivalists: Čelakovský's son, a botanist; Frič; Palacký's son, a geographer known as "the runaway encyclopedia." The students were reared on the liberalism of the day, and my inaugural lecture was on "Hume and Skepticism." The fact that I chose English philosophy and brought up the issue of skepticism created quite a stir. University circles were not pleased by my criticism of Kant and German pro-Kantian philosophy. Yet another unfortunate instance of anti-German patriotism combined with actual dependence on Germans! When one of the students — Jungmann I think it was — asked me to lecture to his club, I spoke on Blaise Pascal as a way of demonstrating that religion was not so dead as German liberalism claimed, that it was a necessity of the human heart. I wanted to deal a blow to all their liberal indifference. The educated man of the day had written religion off and could scarcely understand how anyone could take it seriously.

I was not an enthusiastic teacher; I often disliked lecturing. I am not fond of speaking in public and have to force myself to write. I was not interested in explaining to the boys what others had written and taught. "These are the books on the subject," I would say. "Read them." I preferred to air concrete issues of the day and was happiest when they asked me questions or argued with me. At least I could tell that they were thinking and what they were thinking, and I learned a thing or two as well. When the lecture hall inhibited them, I would invite them to my house. Even so, I found teaching very trying at times. There is great responsibility involved in instructing the young in moral issues. Teaching someone to read and write, imparting general knowledge, and going over what others know is a very different matter from assuming responsibility for the actions of a person who listens to you and takes you as an example, acts in accordance with what you say. As a teacher or writer you are responsible for that person's life. Sometimes on my way to a lecture I was so morally depressed that I got as far as the Clementinum courtyard and couldn't go on — I simply couldn't. I would turn back home and ask the porter to tell the students I was unable to lecture that day.

Perhaps another reason I have never been a true pedagogue is that all my life I have been self-taught. I am an individual and a democrat, both in life and in metaphysics. I believe that all souls are created equal and that each soul belongs to itself, is a law unto itself, independent. People develop side by side, so to speak, each on his own; the only way they can have an effect, a real effect, on one another is by getting to know one another. The most important thing is to look after yourself — keep track of what you do and try to improve — and let others do the same. That is not egoism. On the contrary. What being independent, self-reliant, and self-sufficient actually means is not asking things of others that you can and should do for yourself. There is moral beggary as well as material beggary. I have always wanted everyone to be his own master. Politically, socially, and morally. Being your own master includes both freedom and discipline.

*

There are not many of us left with a clear memory of the eighties in Prague. You think they were great days because you measure them by the great names of Rieger,* Neruda, and Vrchlický, but at the time we were often hampered by petty attitudes and lack of means and people. As I always say when I feel hampered by the limitations of the times, perhaps in fifty years this period will seem so glorious that the people living then will almost envy us.

I am not *laudator temporis acti*, a eulogist of the good old days. Whenever I read that we should return to the ideals of our fathers, I recall what those days were like and realize we're closer to their ideals today. The world is better than it was then, our Czech world in particular. I would punish anyone who moans and groans about the present by setting him back in the eighties. I have lived long enough to say that I believe in the future, in evolution and progress. I should like to see what life will be like a hundred years hence.

Since the war I have slept poorly, and reading through the night is bad for the eyes, so I paint utopias. I imagine the world as it will be in twenty or a hundred years. Mine are practical utopias: I seek out the best there is today and embroider on it a little. The future is with us now. If we choose the best of what we have now, we'll be on the right road; we'll have extended our lives with a piece of the future.

School and Other Interests

When I left Vienna for Prague, I had only my professorial career in mind. I was afraid conflicts would arise, and I would rather have avoided them. I am not a crusader by nature. I never wanted to be in the forefront of political affairs and polemics. As I have said, I was usually dragged into them.

I found the standards at the new Czech University rather low: there was no criticism, no exchange of views. During a lecture Professor Durdík gave to the Philosophical Society, he asked the audience to name the five — I think it was five — greatest philosophers. No one responded. When I said that he must not omit Comte, there was general consternation: how could an *extraordinarius* stand up to an *ordinarius*? The students thought it was a lark, and shortly thereafter a piqued Durdík responded in the press by saying that an American like myself would probably call Barnum the greatest philosopher.

Realizing that we needed an organ of scholarly criticism, I founded the monthly *Athenaeum*. It ran reviews of our own and foreign scholarship and of literature as well: I have always found literature as important a source of knowledge as science. When Professor Pacold of the Technical University received a devastating review of his book on civil engineering, a review written for the *Athenaeum* by several of his colleagues, I, as editor, was raked over the coals. Then a thesis on romantic poetry submitted by the playwright Jeřábek, author of *The Servant of His Master*, for the Chair of Literature was condemned in the *Athenae-um* by a cohort of colleagues as lacking in scholarship. I had no idea that Jeřábek was Rieger's protégé, but Rieger took the criticism as a personal affront and held it against me for a long time to come. One more illustration of what things were like: a certain professor found serious fault with me for publishing reviews of new and foreign works. It didn't do, he said, for students to read about pertinent material before their professors had cited it in their lectures: it undermined the profes-sors' authority. The *Athenaeum* came out for about ten years. It was far from perfect, but it was something at least.

Another problem I noticed was that the new Czech University was not doing enough to promote education among the people. I therefore proposed that it should initiate extension courses for as broad a constituency as possible, and I myself taught such courses and gave lectures. I wrote that we needed a second Czech university. I also felt we needed a new encyclopedia: Rieger's was fine in its day, but it was obsolete. What I had in mind was something like the Encyclopaedia Britannica, and I found collaborators and a publisher. But the Manuscripts Controversy disrupted my work. Besides, I had ideas that some found hard to accept. For example, I proposed that my collaborators should work as hard as they could for a year and then burn all they had written: I thought they needed practice and experience. Well, at least we got the *Otto Encyclopedia* out of it. And in the process I met Jan Laichter, who later published my *Selected Essays* and the journal *Naše doba* (Our Times). I also tried to publish early Czech religious works, that is, the writings of Hus, Štítný, Chelčický, and the like: it wasn't enough to boast about our Hussite past, we needed to know it. But although a society was founded to see to that end, it made no headway. I suppose the Manuscripts Controversy was to blame.

It would never have occurred to me to enter the fray if Gebauer, with whom I'd had little contact before then, hadn't come to me and asked me to print an article in the *Athenaeum* arguing that the Queen's Court and Green Mountain Manuscripts were fabrications of our own century. This is more or less how it happened: Gebauer had set forth his objections to the Manuscripts in some scholarly publication or other, and when Martin Hattala attacked him for it in the press Gebauer wanted to defend himself. Now Kvíčala and Gebauer had their own *Listy filologické* (Philological Papers), but Kvíčala wouldn't publish Gebauer's rebuttal for fear of offending his colleagues. I accepted it of course, partly because I knew what a fine scholar Gebauer was and partly because I did not believe in the authenticity of the Manuscripts myself. I had been somewhat influenced in the matter by Šembera back in Vienna and still more by Vašek's criticisms. I considered the Manuscripts issue to be first and foremost a moral issue: if they were forgeries we had to confess it to the world; our pride, our culture could not be based on a lie. Besides, we could never know our history properly if we kept stumbling over a fancied past. It was perfectly obvious to me.

The result was an affair that dragged on for years. Philologists, historians, paleographers, and chemists all declared the Manuscripts to be counterfeits. I tried to show that for aesthetic and sociological reasons they could not come from the Middle Ages. Hattala opposed us. Kvíčala, who had told Gebauer in private that he didn't believe in their authenticity, turned against us too. Soon the press jumped on the bandwagon — Julius Grégr and the *Národní listy* and the religious press — decrying us as unpatriotic and traitors to the nation. It was all very silly. Then the patriotic clubs lit into us and even the man in the street. One day while waiting for Schwaiger in a pub, I noticed Vojta Náprstek's brother, a brewery owner, sitting at the next table. He didn't know who I was and started going on about me, saying I'd been bribed by the Germans to drag the Czech past through the mud and so on. Well, I let him have his say and even egged him on. It was only after I'd left that they told him he'd been talking about me to myself. Another time I joined some people on a tram cursing that traitor Masaryk. I found it amusing. What made me angry was to see people defending the Manuscripts when they did not believe in them but were afraid to admit it.

One good thing did come of the battles: I was forced to read through the entire literature of the period that gave rise to the Manuscripts, that is, I made a thorough study of the authors of our nationalist revival from Dobrovský* onward — a fine fellow, Dobrovský, highly educated and the first Czech in the modern era with a cosmopolitan outlook. I read Jungmann, Linda, Šafařík. *Ad vocem* Linda: Why didn't our patriots think of publishing his *Glow Above the Heathens* to commemorate the millenary of our patron saint, Saint Wenceslas*? And by the way, the Manuscripts' defenders extolled the pagan era as unspoiled by German influence, yet they joined with us in honoring Saint Wenceslas. We go on about tradition and then fail to recognize it. I carefully perused the literature of the eighteenth and nineteenth centuries for a picture of the times and mood from which the Manuscripts sprang: the romanticism, the historicism, the desire to measure up to other nations and, above all, to the Germans. But the Manuscripts did not only increase my awareness of our national revival; they led me farther into the past, into our history, to the Reformation and Counter-Reformation, and then forward again to the leaders of the National Revival movement: Palacký,* Kollár, Smetana, Havlíček. So for me too the Manuscripts Controversy was a political event: it introduced me to our political problems.

*

Soon thereafter I was involved in another rumpus. A young man by the name of Hubert Gordon Schauer, the son of a half-Czech, half-German family from Litomyšl, had got into trouble in Vienna. He was a Hegelian, and Professor Zába, the philosopher, recommended him to me, asking me to save him for the sake of the Czech nation. Fine. I brought him to Prague and put him up at our place — we were living at Vlček's house in Vinohrady at the time. He turned out to be gifted but unbalanced. He was always off carousing with his friends Mrštík the writer and Štolc the scientist, coming home late at night and climbing over the fence, trampling Vlček's flower beds, making an awful mess, so I had to turn him out. At about that time a group of students close to us younger professors decided they wanted a voice of their own and founded the biweekly *Čas* (Time). The first I heard of it was when I opened the inaugural issue and saw Schauer's article "Our Two Problems." They must have printed it because they hadn't received enough contributions. It was outrageous: an anonymous author wondering whether it wouldn't be better for us Czechs to throw in our lot with the Germans and join in the life of a great *Kulturvolk*, a civilized people. The very next morning I went to have it out with Herben, the editor, and to this day I remember finding him in bed under one of those thick down quilts you see in the country and telling him off. And then *I* was blamed for the article. The writer Ferdinand Schulz hurled a national malediction down upon me in *Národní listy*: I was a philosopher of suicide; our sweet poetess Eliška Krásnohorská went so far as to curse my mother. Later Schauer admitted to having written the article — he too had joined *Národní listy*, as an editor — but the fury roused against me was many years in dying down.

*

At the time I thought it mere chance that I got into such skirmishes, but now I see that the circumstances were such that I couldn't avoid public life and that even from the podium I tried to influence the course it took. When I lectured on Hume and Pascal and made reference to Comte, I was deliberately attempting to bring English and French philosophy into the public eye and free us from our one-sided intellectual subservience to Germany. That is why I had abridged versions of Comte's *Sociology* and Sully's *Psychology* translated and published. My own *Concrete Logic*, written hurriedly during a Hustopeč holiday, was an attempt to bring order and method into the sciences. Scientists tend to go scurrying along like pedestrians with no common goal. They need organization, and organization, like any attempt to overcome anarchy, is *eo ipso* political.

*

The issue that concerned me most at the time was the Slav question. It was something I had thought about — though vaguely and, so to say, instinctively — since childhood. As a boy I puzzled over how I could make out so much of what the Polish uhlans said (they had a camp for a

111

time in Čejkovice) even though they were of a different nation. While at the Gymnasium I studied Polish out of romantic sympathy with the Polish uprising, and in Vienna I set to work on Russian.

As a young man I once spent my holidays on a farm outside the town of Pápa near Lake Balaton in Hungary. At the time I was fascinated by historical atlases: how far the Roman Empire had reached, how deep Svatopluk's realm had penetrated into Pannonia, where the Slavs had settled. I believed the conjectures about Székesfehérvár being Svatopluk's ancient Velehrad and other such flights of fancy. One day I was sitting in front of the local castle poring over one of my atlases — Kipert-Mencken I think it was — when a man came up and engaged me in conversation. The more he talked the more technical he became, until in the end he had torn my Slav fantasies to pieces. He turned out to be Professor Sickel, a famous University of Vienna paleographer and historian, who had come on a visit to the owner of the castle.

Although I had read quite a bit of Russian literature in Vienna, I became completely absorbed in it in Prague. If I do say so myself, hardly anyone there had the knowledge of Russian literature that I had. I'd come across Slavophilism in Kollár and Slavophiles in our political life, but in fact they paid only lip service to the concept and knew nothing about it. So I studied Russian Slavophilism: Kireevsky — Schelling's disciple — and most of all Dostoevsky. From the latter I learned how closely Russian Slavophilism is connected with Orthodoxy. Dostoevsky was an atheist. He once said to the Russian nihilists, "*You* presume to tell *me* what atheism is?" But he *wanted* to be Orthodox, he wanted to "lie his way to the truth." It was a vain hope: you can never return to a lost faith; you can embrace a new one, but you never find the one you've lost. That is why I regarded Dostoevsky's longing for Orthodoxy as a kind of jesuitry. It gave me no peace: I had to see Russia and the Orthodox faith at close quarters.

I first went to Russia in 1887 and returned a year later. I stopped in Warsaw to meet Poles. I visited Petersburg, Moscow, Kiev, and Odessa. It was fascinating to see the streets and places I knew so well from Dostoevsky, Tolstoy, and other writers. I traveled third class on land and in steerage on the Black Sea partly because I wanted to get to know the people and partly because I had little money. I looked up Slav philologists like Lamansky and Florinsky. Lamansky told me straight out that Russians are interested only in the Orthodox Slavs and perhaps the Slovaks, because Slovaks are as naive as the simple Russian folk; the Czechs — liberals and Westernizers all — they would send to the devil. I went to Russian churches and visited shrines and hermitages. At the Sergeev Monastery I was the guest of the father superior and observed Orthodoxy's ignorance and superstition. And that was what the Slavophiles looked to for the salvation of Slavdom! On the whole I left the country with the same feelings as Havlíček before me: love for the Russian people and scorn for official policy and the ruling intelligentsia.

I called on Tolstoy. I had not had time to read him as thoroughly as I had Dostoevsky, so I wanted to get to know him personally. I visited him first in his Moscow residence. I remember as if it were yesterday how he showed me his study with what was almost pride: it had a rustic wooden ceiling that he could touch with his hand, but it had been artificially built into a large, stately room. A peasant hut with a writing desk and a comfortable leather armchair — there was something decidedly wrong there. The study also had a Black Forest wooden clock that he boasted had cost only thirty-five kopeks. He wore a belted *muzhik* shirt and shoes he had made himself — and made badly, of course. For tea he took me into the salon. It was all red velvet, as was the custom among the nobility. His wife, the Countess, served the usual jam, but he pretended not to notice and sipped his tea through a piece of sugar like a *muzhik*. After tea we went into the garden. We talked of Schopenhauer, whom Lev Nikolaevich misunderstood. In the middle of our conversation he stopped like a *muzhik* at the boundary of a field and bade me to do the same. It all seemed forced to me, artificially primitive, unnatural.

Later Lev Nikolaevich invited me to Yasnaya Polyana. I took a *kibitka*, a covered wagon, from Tula. Entering the village, we saw a bridge so dilapidated that our horses would have demolished it. We had to make a detour. I reached the house just before noon. I was told that Lev Nikolaevich was still asleep — he had been up all night debating with his disciple Chernov and some guests — so I took a turn through the village. It was dirty and poverty-stricken. I fell into conversation with a young *muzhik* working in front of a hut and noticed sores under his open shirt: venereal disease. In another hut I found a filthy, helpless old woman sitting on the stove, working herself to death. I went back to the manor house. That day another disciple, the son of the painter Gay, had come to see him. He had simplified his life to such an extent that he made the long journey on foot. Trains are not peasant-like, he claimed. He arrived so full of lice that he had to go at once for a good bath and scrub. Tolstoy told me he would drink from the glass of a syphilitic so as not to show his disgust or humiliate him. Why did he think of that and not of ridding his peasants of the infection? When he began going on about how we must live the simple life, like peasants, I said, "But what about your house with its salon and armchairs and sofas? And the wretched life of your peasants? Is that the simple life? True, you don't drink, but you do smoke cigarette after cigarette. If you're going to be an ascetic, then be thorough about it. But the peasant lives a poor life because he is poor, not to be an ascetic." I also told him what I saw in his village, the disorder, the disease, the dirt. "How in God's name can you fail to see it? You, a great artist, you don't notice it? Making your own shoes, walking instead of traveling by train — what a waste of time! Think of the useful things you could have done instead!" I quoted the English proverb "Cleanliness is next to godliness" and our Czech proverb "Cleanliness is the half of health." But the long and the short of it was that we couldn't see eye to eye. The Countess was a sensible woman and hated to see Tolstoy giving away everything unreasonably; she was thinking of her children. When later she quarreled with Lev Nikolaevich, I couldn't help taking her side.

The third time I visited Tolstoy was shortly before his death in 1910. By that time he had inwardly made a complete break with his wife. He was on edge, unable to control himself. The doctor attending him was a Slovak by the name of Makovický, a man completely devoted to Tolstoy and his teachings. He went about with a piece of pencil lead in his fingernail, scribbling every word Lev Nikolaevich said into a notebook in his pocket. Simplicity! The simple life! Heavens! The town-and-country controversy cannot be resolved by imposing a sentimental moral code and declaring the peasant and rural life the pattern for us all. Agriculture is undergoing industrialization and must have machinery. Today's peasant needs more education than his grandfather did. We too have many false ideas and inherited prejudices on the subject.

But most of all we argued over non-resistance to evil. Tolstoy did not understand that the issue at hand is not merely opposing evil by force but waging an all-out war on it. He failed to make a distinction between defensive and offensive. He thought, for example, that had the Russians not resisted their Tartar invaders they would have abstained from violence after only a brief massacre. My theory is, if a man attacks me with intent to kill, I will defend myself, and if there is no other alternative, I will kill him. If one of us has to die, why not the one with the evil intent?

*

I have no more use for blather about Slavdom than I have for patriotism in general. Tell me, how many of our Slavophiles can read Russian, Polish, Serb? How many of the people who go on about belonging to the Hussite nation have read a page of Hus* or a work on the Hussite Reformation? What's the use of talking, anyway? Your normal individual does not go about trumpeting the fact that he loves his parents, his wife, and his children. It's taken for granted. If you love your country, you don't talk about it, you do something for it. That's all that matters. I know perfectly well how big and how problematic the Slav issue is. I've studied Poland, I've studied Russia, I've been active in Croat and Serb politics; I'm more than half Slovak and had a program for Slovakia more than fifty years ago. And of course I'd never have done it without love; people follow their hearts in these matters and for that very reason say nothing of love but look to their reason for help. I've always tried to avoid the words "my country" and "my people": they give me a sense of shame. I do not cry aloud that I am a patriot or that someone else is a traitor. If I disagree with the road someone has taken, I must argue against it for such and such reasons. Big words can make people drunk; they cannot teach them to work. We have rid ourselves of despotic masters; we must now rid ourselves of despotic words. Granted, people cling to words in all fields — religion, science, philosophy — not only in politics. That is why I have always emphasized things, facts, awareness, observation. But to learn and to learn *well* you need love.

AT WORK AND IN STRIFE

Politics

I have always been interested in politics. Even the village brawls between Slovaks and Hanáks and later, at the Brno Gymnasium, between Czechs and Germans were politics in miniature, and I had to come to grips with the relations between them. Likewise, my desire to become a diplomat was as much the result of a vague interest in politics as it was romantic. But my relationship to politics has been theoretical as well: I was fascinated by Plato's political philosophy, and as soon as I took up sociology I was inevitably involved in political issues. I found economics fascinating too and, as I've said, attended lectures by Menger in Vienna and by Roscher in Leipzig; as a student I dipped into the second edition of Marx's *Capital*.

Naturally I've always reacted to political events. My first articles, written for *Moravské orlice* (The Moravian Eagle) while I was still a student, were a condemnation of political passivity. In Vienna I went to the railway station to watch the arrival of the Czech members of Parliament and kept a close watch on conflicts between Czechs and Germans, but early on I realized the real conflict was with Austria, and my attitude to Austria was decidedly negative.

When I first arrived in Prague, I was full of cultural and scholarly interests: the *Athenaeum*, the Czech University, the encyclopedia, the Manuscripts Controversy, and the journalistic and political activity connected with the latter. Revising the picture of our supposed ancient Slav culture meant revising the picture of our present-day cultural life. Then came the journal *Čas* (Time) and the furor caused by Schauer. These were the conflicts and polemics that drew me into active politics. I saw our mistakes and the low level of our journalism and public opinion, but I also saw fine, decent people. The fact that I aroused such fury and hostility — often against my will and sometimes from sheer stupidity — even turned out to my advantage. At the time I said to myself, "You deserve it for getting mixed up in these things!" But today I see that hatred too gives a person fame and respect. The hatred passes, but the name associated with it remains in people's minds. I still tell this to people forced to defend themselves on all sides.

At first there were only a few of us, a small group of professors that included Kaizl, Kramář, and — to some extent — Heyrovský and Rezek. People thought of Goll as one us, but he wasn't. We had nothing you could call a political program; we simply held together as a generation. We wanted to better things, reform the press and the University, take a positive, active role in politics. Ours was more of a critical, scholarly movement than a clear-cut platform. Kaizl was an economist; Kramář was at work on an excellent study of the Czech High Court and its activities in Vienna before it was abolished under Maria Theresa. When Pazdírek wrote an article about our group for his *Slavische Warte* (The Slav Viewpoint) and gave it to me in manuscript, I noticed that he called us "positivists." I found the term too redolent of Comte, of French and other varieties of positivism. I told him he would do better to use "realists." That is how we came by the name.

Pazdírek wanted us to join the Old Czech Party and talked it over with Rieger. Naive and good-natured as he was, he promised more to Rieger than we could deliver. I was friends with Bráf and Bráf knew Rieger's family, so he introduced me to Rieger and Mattuš and they started dealing with us directly. Rieger was decent to me despite our former differences, and we got on well together. We prepared a statement of the conditions according to which we were willing to join the Party, but the demand that we should have the main say in the Party press did not sit well with the Old Czech journalists, and when they — especially the *Hlas národa* (Voice of the Nation) staff — started getting their knives into us, the whole thing came to nought.

Then — in 1899, I believe — the Young Czechs won at the polls. *De facto* there was less of a difference between them and the Old Czechs than their skirmishes in the press might have led one to believe. Even some members of our Realist group thought along Old Czech lines. I used to say that Kaizl was an Old Czech Realist, Kramář a Young Czech

Realist, and I a realistic Realist. Since the Young Czechs were gaining in popularity, they needed new blood for Parliament. They wanted us to join their Party, and we felt it our duty to accommodate them. On the whole the Old Czechs had better and better-educated people, but they were politically rigid. Jan Kučera, the lawyer, promoted our membership, as did Václav Škarda, a member of the Diet with whom I was in touch. And so we joined. A fair-minded statement in *Národní listy* (National News) and *Čas* (Time) put an end to our former enmity, and at the next parliamentary elections, in 1891, I was elected as a member of the Young Czech Party for Southern Bohemia.

The guiding light, the *spiritus rector* of the Young Czech Party was Dr. Engel, a physician. Although he drew up every agenda and was perfectly decent and sensible, he kept in the background, hardly ever appearing in public. Then there were the two Grégrs: Dr. Julius Grégr, who edited *Národní listy,* and Dr. Edvard Grégr, who was a member of Parliament, an orator, and a good man, though sometimes his temperament made the welkin ring with radical flights that he himself had to laugh at afterwards; the patriarch Alois Trojan, an ex-Old Czech and a straightforward, dignified man; Dr. Josef Herold, a magnificent orator and herald and standard-bearer of the Party and thus worthy of his name; and Ervin Špindler, a fine man, bearded like an apostle, with whom I would argue about liberalism and atheism and who couldn't understand how an educated man could be religious. The radical wing included Dr. Edvard Brzorád and Jan Vašatý, the brother of my former Piarist teacher at the Hustopeč *Realschule.* Vašatý made the Party's Slav policy, though he had precious little knowledge of Slavdom. He mistrusted us, and when I had a run-in with the Party he sided against me. Dr. Pacák didn't come to the fore until later. Still, we Realists were generally well received. Only Eim, the Vienna correspondent of *Národní listy,* was annoyed each time I scored a success in Parliament. He started out strongly in favor of me, but soon behaved more like an enemy.

What I found most interesting in the Vienna Parliament was the Parliament itself. I had read through the Constitution and Rules of Procedure several times over, but — believe me — there was as great a difference between the Constitution and parliamentary practice as there is between the Gospels and the Church. I kept my eyes open and my thoughts to myself. The government dais was like an altar, and we down below were meant to be the believers. I soon discovered that Parliament had a fine library. I attended all meetings I possibly could, and read political literature during them. I was politically immature and extremely inexperienced, though as an orator I had some success speaking on education and leading the attack against Minister Kállay for his treatment of Bosnia and Herzegovina. That gained me the friendship of the Serb and Croat members of Parliament, and I traveled through Bosnia and Herzegovina tailed by Kállay's spies. Once I so provoked Menger, a German, that he called me a traitor. There was a great to-do about it, and Menger was reprimanded and had to apologize to me before the whole House.

After a number of skirmishes I had a major conflict with the Party. This is how it happened: the first time I spoke to Thun in the Diet in Prague, he insulted the Czechs to my face, saying that a Czech is either a lout or a lickspittle. Naturally I repeated his dictum to various and sundry people, and it caused a dreadful row. The Young Czechs were annoyed with me for not having informed them about it, though in fact I had mentioned it to Tilscher, who apparently forgot. Then an anonymous and highly acrimonious article attacking Julius Grégr appeared in *Čas* in connection with the affair, and Grégr, thinking I had written it, went after me. I told no one who the real author was, thus preserving editorial confidentiality. Not even Dr. Kramář knew. (Only recently has it become common knowledge that the article was by Kaizl.) The Party was clearly in a bad way and handled the affair by making a nasty statement that could only have referred to me, though it did not refer to me by name. I went to my constituency, got a vote of confidence, and with that in my pocket wrote to our members of Parliament in Vienna resigning my mandate. Maybe I should have consulted with the col-leagues in our group beforehand, but I often made up my mind on the spur of the moment. Kaizl and Kramář remained in the Party. I disliked the Party's two-faced approach: it was one thing in Prague and another in Vienna. At home the members of Parliament ranted and raved, while in Vienna they gave in to the government in return for minor conces-sions. I also had a different attitude towards the Germans. But most of all I realized I was still politically weak.

Not that I gave up politics when I resigned. On the contrary. I wanted to start from scratch; I wanted to come up with a new kind of politics, a revivalist politics, and make a dent in the minds of our people. I devoured Czech political literature from the eighteenth century onwards. I found Dobrovský particularly attractive for his keen intellect and outlook on the world. In politics my teacher was Palacký: he is the basis for my whole humanitarian program. I also admired Havlíček for his truthfulness and openness; he taught me how to write journalism. I read Kollár, Rieger — everybody. The main fruit of my studies was *The Czech Question*, an unfinished piece of work, no more than a collection of material, but *Havlíček* and *Our Current Crisis* also date from this period.

I've always been a reluctant writer: I'd have much preferred not to publish at all; I never polish or refine enough. The only reason I wrote the books was that I felt they had something to say to their time. If people had left me alone — and I them — I daresay I'd never have published a thing. Once I joined the fray, I occasionally laid about me more than necessary, giving offense, true, but receiving even more. I often turned my nose up at people and could be rather high-and-mighty, but my greatest fault was impatience: I felt people should accept a good cause at once and act on it. I have had spats all my life, though I don't think I'm combative by nature. I never fought for the sake of fighting, but when provoked I defended myself. Even a literary battle has its uses: it may blind you, but it also makes you think — you and your enemy. I believe that all the conflicts helped to build our national consciousness and deepen our spiritual life.

Considering the quantity of books and pamphlets I've published, it's odd I never really wanted to write. Nor, as I've said, did I ever have an inclination for teaching. Furthermore, believe me, I dislike appearing in public. Left to my own devices, I'd have been satisfied to read and study and if to write, then for myself — in short, to learn. I am interested in everything: all the sciences, all the issues and missions of our times. I am happy if I can read in quiet, and I am a voracious reader to this day. I don't like meeting people: I am shy. Each new acquaintance, even a formal one, is work, and this has made politics and public activity harder for me than for most people. Why have I done it then? Because I had to.

That's easy to say, of course, but I don't mean it as an excuse or an apology. You can see from all my books, pamphlets, and articles, from my every move, that I've never become involved in anything I didn't find crucial and directly relevant to my own life. Since coming to Prague in 1882, I have amassed an enormous amount of experience. I am grateful to fortune for granting me so full a life.

The Nineties

Looking back on the nineties, I see what a time of ferment it was. The nineties in a broad sense, I mean. Take the development of political parties, for instance. Earlier we had really only two: the Old Czechs and the Young Czechs. The Old Czechs were on their way down at the time: theirs was the decline of the old bourgeois patricians. The Young Czechs were the party of the new, rising class, more rural and more radical. In 1889 and then again in 1891 the Young Czechs had a majority over the Old Czechs in the Diet and in Parliament. Until then our politics had been what would today be called bourgeois, and suddenly it began to break down according to class.

A philosopher by the name of Alfons Šťastný organized an agrarian wing within the ranks of the Young Czechs. He was a kind of pundit of the people, an atheist and disciple of the German materialism of Vogt, Moleschott, and Büchner. I made fun of his ideas, which I imagine is why he had a grudge against me.

Then there was socialism. *De facto* we had had it earlier, its tentative beginnings going back to the Christian Socialism of 1848. But gradually, as industry developed, the number of workers increased, and by the nineties, under the influence of the Viennese Socialists, a strong Social Democratic Party started growing on a Marxist base. To oppose it, Klofáč organized the Nationalist Workers within the Young Czech Party, but they soon split off on their own. I had dealings with them — mostly with Choc — and soon tussles as well.

I've been interested in socialism all my life. In Brno I observed Christian Socialism, and in Vienna I read Marx and the Catholic Socialists. Schauer wrote his first articles for a journal run by a prominent Christian Socialist by the name of Vogelsang. I once visited my friend Hanuš Schwaiger when he was painting Saint George at the Castle at Průhonice, and there I met the German Christian Socialist Dr. Mayer at the house of Count Sylva-Taroucca, whom I had known in Parliament.

During the nineties I started having practical contact with socialism. I spent a lot of time with working people and gave talks to them. When strikes broke out in Prague and Kladno, I set up a series of lectures for the strikers and delivered some myself. I wanted to put something other than hunger and poverty into their heads. To Steiner and others I proposed a Workers Academy, where laborers and the newspapermen who wrote about them could get a political education. During the 1905 drive for universal suffrage I addressed a public rally in Haymarket Square and marched in the demonstration with my wife. Even before then I had been written and spoken of as a socialist, and caricatures always showed me wearing the socialist slouch hat. In those days the word "socialist" was like a bogeyman to the middle classes and intelligentsia. I accepted socialism insofar as it coincided with my humanitarian program. Marxism I did not accept. My *Social Question* was meant to be a critique of Marx. When the Czech Socialists entered the Parliament in Vienna, they refused to subscribe to the declaration of *Staatsrecht*, national law, made by the other Czech parties. The result was a great hue and cry, and they were branded traitors. I stood up for them and had to pay the consequences, of course, though the founders of the Young Czech Party had invoked natural law, as I did then, along with historical law.

*

My socialism is simply a matter of loving your neighbor, of humanity. I don't want there to be poverty, I want everyone to live decently, in and by his own labor, and to have enough elbowroom, as the Americans say. Loving your neighbor is not old-style philanthropy; philanthropy only helps here and there. A real love of humanity seeks to amend conditions by law and deed. If that is socialism, I am for it.

I do not believe in equality, absolute equality, that is. There is no equality in the stars or in man. There always have been and always will be individuals who by their own gifts and a combination of circumstances not of their own making can and do achieve more than others; there will always be a hierarchy among people. But hierarchy means order, organization, discipline, knowledge, and obedience, not the exploitation of man by man. That is why I do not accept Communism. No sooner did Lenin take power than he called for leaders. The longer I live, the more I realize the role played by the individual in the evolution of humanity, but I repeat: more talent and more of what is known as luck do not justify the exploitation of the less gifted and less fortunate. I do not believe that all private ownership can be done away with. The personal relationship — the *pretium affectionis* — that binds an owner to his property is good in that it promotes economic progress. Communism is possible, but only among brothers, that is, in the family or in a religious community or close circle of friends; it can be maintained only by true love. I do not accept the principle of class war. There are social estates and social classes, there are degrees of difference among people. But that does not mean war; it means the organization of natural inequality and of inequality resulting from historical circumstance, it means leveling, growth, and development. I am not so blind and simple-minded as to fail to see injustice and oppression, and I know that individuals, estates, and classes must protect their own interests, but it does not follow that *homo homini lupus*, man is a wolf to man, as was said long ago.

As for Marxism, it is an economic theory and philosophy, a philosophy of history in particular. Economic theory, like every science, is a matter for investigation, revision, and improvement, and Marxism, like any philosophy, must be open to criticism and free deliberation. That is why revisionism arose and will continue to do so. Every revision of a creed or program is painful, but without the pain there can be no progress. I have no ready-made social doctrine in my pocket. As I've said elsewhere, I am always for the workman and working people in general, often for socialism, and rarely for Marxism.

My views of socialism derive from my concept of democracy. A revolution or a dictatorship can occasionally abolish bad things, but it never creates anything good and lasting. Impatience is fatal in politics. When I consider that all recorded human history goes back only some ten thousand years and that we are still on the threshold of civilization, how can I believe that a fanatic, despot, or revolutionary will complete our development at one stroke? Serfdom and slavery were done away with less than two hundred years ago, forced labor even more recently, and it is only for the past hundred, no, even fifty years that we have worked consciously and systematically on the social problems of working people and the lower classes in general. We have hundreds of thousands, millions of years ahead of us. Must we really do everything at once? In any case, you can't feed the hungry on the future. Faith in development and progress does not free us from tending to the needs of today.

*

Although the more radical strain in the Young Czech Party won out, Party leaders failed to grasp the pressing need to shape the nation according to its increasingly specialized movements and parties. Instead of becoming a truly national organization, they opposed all new trends and parties.

Unlike the Young Czechs I strove to create a movement or party that might be called organizational, a party of "realism." The Young Czechs failed to comprehend it, of course, and thus opposed it bitterly. And even if after their 1891 victory they accepted us three magi of Realism, it could not last.

What about the movement known as Youth? It was a kind of synthesis of Young Czechs and Realism. It was made up of young people for whom Realism was too academic, not national enough. In 1893 a group of them — including Čížek, Rašín, the Hajns, Sokol, and Soukup — was tried for high treason. It was a stupid move on Austria's part, as stupid as the war-time trial of Dr. Rašín and Dr. Kramář. I regarded those young people's radicalism as ill-conceived; I could see they were unprepared to take any serious action. They were the ones I had in mind when I came up with the slogan "Revolution is philistinism." I was incensed at the murder of the poor cripple, whether or not he was actually in the pay of the police. Yet I defended them within the Young Czech Party, which had disowned them.

Čížek, the leader of the movement and a sensible fellow, worked for *Národní listy*. The member of the group I knew best was Stanislav Sokol. His father, a teacher and Young Czech, was a fine man and a preacher in the Comenius mold. He lived opposite us on Sokol Street. Věra Hurbanová, the daughter of the Slovak poet Vajanský, was living with us at the time I was promoting closer ties with Slovaks, and she made friends with the Sokols. It was through her that our families met. I remembered having known Stanislav when he was a student at the University. He had been brought before the faculty for some reason or other — he was a handsome boy with a pale, transparent face — and I took his part. During the Youth trial I disagreed with the way the defense was managed, thus incurring the wrath of Dr. Rašín, Čížek's comrade and fellow-victim. But I valued Rašín's matter-of-factness and refused to take offense at his brusque manner. I later sent books to him and his Bory prisonmates. Russian literature mostly.

The Radical Progressive Party developed out of the youth move- ment. Hořínek, the brother-in-law of the poet Machar, edited their paper *Pokrokové listy* (Progressive News) together with Pelc, Antonín Hajn, the writer Šlejhar, and a few others. I debated with them at Hořínek's, but we never did understand one another. Stanislav Sokol decided to publish a series of translations, and for a time I served as an adviser to him. The first book he brought out was Mill's *The Subjection of Women*; it was translated by my wife and her Czech teacher, Miss Blažková, the mathe- matician's sister.

Although I didn't realize it at the time, I was rather unfair to those young people: I didn't know that twenty years later I myself would set out on the road of revolution.

*

It was a time of great ferment in literature as well. We were flooded with foreign literature: French writers from Zola to the symbolists, the Scandinavians and the beginnings of Ibsen's influence. Machar and his *Confession* were typical of the groundswell. Vilém Mrštík promoted

Russian literature, and I lent him Russian critics to write about. Russian literature, Tolstoy and Dostoevsky in particular, had begun to have an effect. All at once there were new impressions and standards. The Czech University played an important role because it was national. Realism stressed the scientific method as an important component of nationalism. In short, the nineties were a potent and vital time. Someone should write a history of the decade, showing how things developed and interacted. Yes, it was a time that combined throwing the windows open on the world and looking deep into ourselves.

When the *Athenaeum* ceased publication, I founded *Naše doba* (Our Times). Laichter's new publishing house had started disseminating scientific and philosophical works. As for politics, after two years of experience in the Vienna Parliament, I decided to study the development of Czech parties and Czech politics in general since 1848. A curious thing happened as I read Havlíček: I kept finding he had written nearly everything I wanted to say about politics. In Palacký's historical works I found a reasoned philosophical justification for the Palacký political program along with his conception of the Czech question and his appre-ciation of the Czech Reformation and humanitarian ideal. His philosophy of history came out most clearly in the pamphlet against Höfler. The closeness I felt to Palacký and Havlíček led me to believe I was on the right track. Politics must be based on a broad historical context, taking into account not only the immediate past but all history. I would add that in politics too the mills of God grind slowly, yet they grind exceeding fine and for all eternity.

*

The campaign surrounding the Hilsner affair was a bad business: it meant doing battle with superstition about ritual murder. I took little interest in the trial until a former student of mine, a Moravian writer by the name of Sigismund Münz, came from Vienna and prevailed upon me to make a statement. I knew the books by the Berlin theologian Starck dealing with the origins and history of ritual superstition and gave my opinion on the matter to Münz. He made it public in the *Neue Freie Presse* and suddenly I landed in the midst of the mêlée. Vienna's anti-

Semites set the Czech nationalist and clerical press on me, and when they attacked, well, I was forced to defend myself, wasn't I? And having taken the first step, I had to go on. That meant studying criminology and physiology, all of which I wrote about in great detail. When I traveled to Polná to inspect the scene of the crime and its surroundings, they said I'd been bribed by the Jews. A group of non-students came to my lectures to shout me down. While they shouted, I wrote a protest against their stupid calumnies on the blackboard, calling upon them to give me the reasons for their demonstration. (Only one of them did so; he came to see me that afternoon, a slender, decent young man who later became the poet Otakar Theer.) To make certain the demonstrators did not think I was afraid of them, I walked all around the lecture hall, challenging them to argue their points; no one dared. And how did the University react? Instead of taking a strong stand and restoring order, it suspended my lectures for a fortnight. That evening the demonstrators came to my house. I was in bed with a chill, so my wife went down to them and told them I was ill but if they wanted to speak to me they could send up a delegation. No one came. I felt very bad about the affair not so much for myself as for the low level of it all. Yet during the war I came to realize how useful it had been. The world press is partly managed or financed by Jews; they knew me from the Hilsner case and repaid me by writing sympathetically about our cause — or fairly at least. That helped us a great deal politically.

*

Ad vocem politics: it may be true that I'm a born politician. At any rate, everything I've ever done and found interesting has had at least an indirect connection with politics. But I've never found political activity satisfying in itself, whether the issues at stake are national or social or anything you may name. I've always opposed philistinism and rowdyism in politics and called for honesty and common sense. That was what I meant when I said that even independence would not save us. In politics I saw only the means; the end for me was religious and moral. But I saw we needed to be politically free to go our own spiritual way. Even today I refuse to claim that the state is the be-all and end-all of our cultural mission. We must prepare the way for the *Civitas Dei*, the Kingdom of God.

Slovakia

I am actually half Slovak: my father was a Slovak from Kopčany and spoke Slovak till the day he died. My childhood language was more Slovak than Czech, unaware as I was of the difference between Slovak-speaking Hungarian Slovaks and Czech-speaking Moravian Slovaks while growing up among them as a child. My Kopčany grandmother would bring me baggy white Slovak trousers as a present when she came to see us, but I wore them only to bed, because otherwise I dressed, as they said at the time, "like a gentleman." The family was in constant contact with Kopčany and Holič, and in Kopčany I heard Hungarian as a child. A few Hungarian words even made their way into our speech at home: we would say *Hallgass* (Be quiet), for example. One or two offspring on my father's side became quite Magyarized, and some cousins from Hungary would come to see me even after I'd moved to Prague. In Vienna I traced the paths of the Slovaks who had lived there, men like Kollár and Kuzmány, the latter being the first, I believe, to attempt a novel in Slovak.

In Prague I attended the meetings held by my Czech University colleagues at the Hotel de Saxe. During the discussions I kept raising the point that we Czechs should work towards political union with the Slovaks. Rezek and Goll and the lawyers Ott and Randa opposed me, citing Rieger's statement to the effect that the Slovak question was a *causa finita*, a closed book. They considered it a matter of historical *Staatsrecht*, national law: they claimed the Czech state consists *de jure* of the historical lands of Bohemia, Moravia, and Silesia; they rejected Slovakia. That's why I questioned their exclusively historical approach. What is historical law anyway? Is the law dependent on time and whether it has actually been put in practice? Isn't law simply law whether or not it has taken effect? Couldn't Austria and the Hungarians turn historical law against us? I have never rejected what is known as historical law, but I combine it with natural law. In the first place, that is more democratic: law is not a hereditary privilege; it is the claim of every nation and every individual to its own life. In the second place, I was concerned for Slovakia: according to historical national law, we should have left Slovakia to the Hungarians. And lastly I disliked the idea of historical law because the concept came out of post-revolution-ary, reactionary Germany. During their early years, the Young Czechs were quite justified in citing natural law side by side with historical law. There were a number of Slovakophiles among us at the time — Heyduk, for example — people with a consciousness of national unity or brother-hood, but it was more a matter of literature than politics: they didn't dare carry it to its political conclusion. The Kollár spirit was still appar-ent in all this, Kollár being content with national and cultural indepen-dence. Neither he nor his contemporaries ever so much as dreamed of political independence.

What concerned me most at the time was that the Czechs and the residents of Prague should really get to know Slovakia. I didn't feel singing Slovak songs was enough. So when we took over *Čas* (Time), I made certain we should have a regular section devoted to Slovakia. I also invited Slovak students — Kukučín, Šrobár, I think, and others — to come and see me. In the late eighties I started renting a summer place in Bystrička near Turčanský Svatý Martin with the conscious goal of getting to know the Slovaks better and having an influence on them. I went there for more than ten years.

Those were the days when even Hurban-Vajanský was a Czecho-phile; later he succumbed to raving Russophilism and looked exclusively to Russia for the redemption of the Slovaks. I was on friendly terms with him, Škultéty, and others. Many Czechs besides myself made their way to Svatý Martin: Věšín, who might even be called the Slovaks' official painter, Schwaiger, and the writer Ignát Herrmann, whom I first met there. The Hungarian police were ready to haul me in when I spoke about Kollár on the site where his house had stood in Mošovce.

Some time in the late 1890s there was a meeting of Slovaks in Svatý Martin. The opposition — the younger wing: Vavro Šrobár, Dušan Petrovič Makovický, and Augustin Ráth — came to see me in Bystrička, and we talked over the Slovak cultural and political platform. The result, in 1898, was a new Slovak review, *Hlas* (The Voice). It was chiefly the work of Šrobár, Pavel Blaho, Makovický (who later became Tolstoy's doctor), and to some extent Milan Hodža. They were opposed by Vajanský, the Catholics with Hlinka at their head, and even the Protestants and Janoška. Slovak life started picking up, and more and more Slovak organizations came into being.

By the time I was ready to go abroad in 1914, I felt I could count on Slovakia, but to act more or less as a plenipotentiary I wanted to know what other members of Parliament and politicians had to say on the matter and therefore sounded them out. I talked specifically to Antonín Hajn, a specialist in constitutional law. He grasped my point immediately and told me he knew an officer on the General Staff who could draw us a map of the future Slovakia, taking into account national, strategic, and similar factors. He went so far as to bring me a map with the future borders penciled in. The present borders are practically identical with the ones on that map.

Once abroad, I was glad to find that the Slovak Štefánik had initiated the same sort of work with the same goal. We were soon joined by others, such as Osuský in America and Pavlů and young Hurban in Russia.

*

When people in Bystrička told me that there were bears roaming the mountains and that they came down to the fields after livestock and oats, I didn't believe it; I thought the shepherds themselves sometimes killed or sold a sheep and laid the blame on bears. Then our neighbor Markovický took me to see what a bear can do. It sits on its hind-quarters in an oat field crushing the oats into its mouth with its fore-paws, dragging itself on its rear through the whole field, and by the time it has finished, the field looks completely trampled. The field Markovický showed me was strewn with what are called "treasures" of oats and blueberries left behind by the bear. "All right," I thought, "if we've got a bear, let's do something about it."

My friends lent me a huge gun, a breechloader from the Turkish Army, and three of us — Markovický, the local forester, and I — went one evening at full moon to lie in wait for it. We waited for an hour or two in a clearing at the edge of the woods adjoining the field, but no bear. It was close to midnight, the stars were shining, and shepherds' fires were burning all along the grassy uplands, here and there and over yonder — a beautiful sight! We forgot about the bear and fell into conversation, Mr. Markovický lighting his pipe, the forester dozing off. And suddenly I sighted it lumbering out of the woods and across the clearing some thirty to thirty-five paces away. It was a giant of a beast and handsome! I picked up my gun, but couldn't shoot: I was trembling like a leaf. Meanwhile the bear had got wind of us. It bounded into the oats and from there back to the woods. Why did I behave so shamefully? It wasn't fear; no, it was more amazement at there actually being such things as bears, as if I hadn't believed they existed, or maybe excitement at its being so strong and handsome a beast that to shoot at it seemed an act of treachery.

The second time I lay in wait for a bear in the woods, the bear turned out to be smaller. I shot it in the chest. It ran a little way, still alive, so we sat down and waited as long as our dog barked at him. Once the dog stopped barking, we went to fetch it. I still have its hide somewhere at home.

The third time I met a bear it happened like this: I was about to leave Bystrička and return to Prague, and went out alone to take my leave of the uplands. I had a rifle and a dog, a brave little tyke, and as we were walking along what did I spy about two hundred paces away but another gigantic beast munching blueberries. I drew closer against the wind, so it wouldn't catch scent of me. But the dog ran ahead, and the bear sniffed it and lunged at it. Because it raised its head, I had to shoot quickly at about a hundred and twenty paces. I wounded it in the chest and it toppled over, but it managed to run into the woods. I took off after it. I knew you don't chase a wounded bear, but I forgot. No, all you can think of at a time like that is bagging your prey. It was bleeding and fled further and further into the hills. I chased it and chased it, but never caught up; it was dark by then. Early the following morning we went out in search of it, trailing its tracks to the boundary of the hunting grounds; farther than that we could not go. I later heard they'd found it the next day in the neighboring hunting grounds dead, already prey to worms. People say bears are like the people from the region where they live; in Slovakia bears are good-natured.

I have hunted wild boars as well, but no other animals. I used to enjoy fishing, though, especially for trout and grayling. It wasn't so much for the fish as for wading in the water and spending hours on the banks of a stream. Any place with trout is beautiful. I taught the people of Svatý Martin to fly-fish. Worms are ugly, and you have to sit in one place with them, while with a fly you can walk where you please. First you choose an artificial fly according to the actual flies in season, then you tie the fly to the line and cast it to the fish, and when a fish bites you hook it quickly and carefully, reel it in, and bag it. It's an art. I usually threw the fish I caught back into the water.

Later I gave it up. My wife felt sorry for the animals.

*

Whenever I'm in nature, I notice how decisive a child's first impressions are throughout his life. I was born on the plains. To this day I don't care for mountains or forests: I find them oppressive somehow. No, give me plains, the sea, the steppe, and if hills there must be, then let me be on the top looking down. Plains have the most beautiful sunsets. I've seen several so breathtaking that they have remained with me all my life. One was in New Jersey, the other in Olomouc. I remember viewing the Prague Castle from the Eliška Bridge through the twilight mist — an exquisite image — and standing on the Legions Bridge and watching the silver light of morning stream up from under the Palacký Bridge. Unforgettable. One winter I was on a train going through a tunnel, and just as we came out I caught sight of a tree with all its leaves: the tunnel had protected it. It was gone before I knew it, but it was like a revelation. In that split second I understood pantheism, the divine in nature. Understood it, though I've never accepted it.

I prefer the country to the town. My four years abroad were all the harder for me because I was forced to live in large cities. When I returned from the war, I noticed that my love for the country had increased. Perhaps improved communications will facilitate the deurbanization called for by socialists. Then not even industry will be crowded into cities and cities will be healthier. Even civilization can bring people closer to nature.

I haven't got your eye; I don't look for details in nature. I look for the whole, the hues and shape of a landscape. I love the sun, fresh air, wind — freedom. You tell me I'm always gazing into the distance. That may be so. I scarcely notice my domestic surroundings. I couldn't tell you how my house at Topol'čianky is furnished. But I do know every last hill on the horizon. I've ridden up all of them on my old horse Hector to see what lies on the other side.

Every time I look at a flower, an insect, or a bird, I want to know everything there is to know about it. Unfortunately I haven't the time. All my time goes to people. It's an occupational hazard. I'm happy in nature, but even in nature I think of people.

1900 to 1910

You ask what I did in my fifties. Well, nothing really. At least I had some peace. I had put those ugly controversies behind me. There was the campaign for the eight-hour working day and the drive for universal suffrage, so of course I did my bit. There were my lectures at the University, though I can't quite recall what they were about. I do know they dealt with social conditions — especially the course in practical philosophy — and my lecture hall was always full even though I was not a good teacher. There were meetings and extension classes, public debates, and suchlike.

It may be a weakness, but I am shy. As I've said before, I don't like speaking in public, and whenever I give a lecture or a speech I have stage fright. Think of all the times I've done it and I still get stage fright when I have to appear in public. Of course if you're just talking to talk — the art of gab for its own sake — there's nothing to it, but talking about practical things, things that have to get done, that's something else again.

I've never enjoyed being number one in the eyes of the public; two or three is quite enough for me. I didn't push my way into public affairs and was reluctant when asked by others to join them. But even when I did so unwillingly and with the feeling I was wasting my time, there was some logic to it; it led to something. Such has always been the case.

*

Early one morning in about 1902 I had a visit from an American with an introduction from Louis Léger in Paris. Until he told me what he wanted, I thought he was a journalist in need of information and I was going over in my mind how much to give him. Instead, he turned out to be a Chicago industrialist by the name of Charles Crane. Mr. Crane had a factory in Russia and, having spent some time there, was interested in the Slavs. He had earmarked funds for Slavic studies at the University of Chicago and was in Prague to invite me to lecture there. He had already invited the Russian liberal Milyukov and several others. I decided to go. I gave a series of ten or twelve lectures on Dostoevsky, Kireevsky, and our own problems. I also traveled about and spoke to our fellow countrymen living there. Crane knew Professor Wilson, and his son served as Secretary of State when Wilson became president; the Cranes helped us a great deal during the war. I returned to America in 1907 to lecture at a congress of nondenominational religious workers. I later lectured again to our Czechs, in particular to the Freethinkers Society in Chicago, which published several of the talks in book form.

I went to England once or twice as well. An off-the-cuff speech I'd given at a teetotaler's conference in Vienna attracted the attention of some of the English delegates, and I got to know a number of English professors and journalists. Later I went to England with my daughter Alice, and we visited Elizabeth Blackwell, a remarkable woman who has opened the path for women in the medical profession. When I returned during the war, I had quite a few friends there.

*

No, I did not found the Progressive or, as it was called at the time, the Realist Party; on the contrary, I opposed it. I wanted to sway public opinion through the press alone or promote a kind of Fabian movement, which would have used lectures and debates to affect all parties. But the young people decided to start their own party because there was no room for them in the others, and when they met and invited me to join, I did. That was in 1900. At their first meetings they put together a platform and published it as *The Red Book*. The Realists were actually more than a political party; they did not only deal with day-to-day politics, theirs was a movement as well, a critical and scientific movement, making our public life more rigorous, more culturally sophisticated, turning it into what I called then a politics of the non-political.

I have joined only two parties in my life: the Young Czech Party as a Realist and the Realist Party. I am not a party man. Not that I don't admit the need for parties, but I've always striven to reform those that exist. I have succeeded to some extent, but at the cost of locking horns with the status quo. I came to Prague a stranger, and a stranger I long remained. That at least in part explains my unique position.

We Czechs started off with one party, the nameless party of Palacký and Havlíček, but a rift developed with the rise of the rural lawyers. During the Young Czech period provincial towns awakened from their provincial slumber; new men burst onto the scene, their sleeves rolled up for action. That's where the Young Czech radical branch came from.

Socialism was the result of industrialization, the crowding together of people of the same background and with the same needs under a factory roof. Socialism developed everywhere — in Germany, France, England, Russia — but the Young Czechs failed to understand it and dealt themselves a blow by trying to deal blows to the Socialists. And besides the worker we had the farmer, an individualist in economic affairs and a conservative for those times.

Add the Catholics and you get four parties altogether: the two large ones (the Socialists and the Agrarians), the "Bourgeois" Party, and the Catholic Party. But specialization or, if you like, fragmentation did not end here; other small parties came into being as well.

The multi-party system is a natural development in politics, but like everything human it has its good and its bad sides. Anything can be abused; the deciding factor is whether people are decent and well educated. I for my part have more faith in people than in institutions, that is, political parties. I find it interesting that we should have created so many parties while the English and Americans get by with two or three. It's not a specifically Czech situation: the German parties here in Czechoslovakia are just as divided. In both instances the fragmentation has its origins in Vienna: Vienna ruled and administered; Parliament and the Diets were controlled by government and crown, so parties bore no real responsibility and the government did not care if they split. We are still in the grip of this bit of Austrian training. Much as we call for de-Austrianization, we are to some extent living in the same old way. But it is important that after the coup the smaller parties came together and a national democracy took shape, that we are beginning to think in terms of larger blocs and thus showing a greater sense of what constitutes a state. Statesmen are politicians and public figures who factor the interest of the state into everything they do. For them the only true form of politics consists in organizing parts into a whole and uniting all efforts. It is a politics that transcends state borders and the politics our postwar era demands.

*

I have felt close to newspapers, the literary organ of politics, all my life. I'd probably be a newspaperman today if I hadn't found another job. Even back in my student days I wrote for the Czech press from Vienna under the initially, and in 1885 or so I asked Dr. Julius Grégr to let me do a science column for the *Národní listy* (National News). At about that time I wrote an article for the German magazine *Politik*: "Mehr Gewerbebildung" (More Vocational Training) I believe it was called. (I can't recall why I wanted to have it in the German press; perhaps someone commissioned it.) Dr. Grégr made a big fuss about it, regarding it as a breach of my contract with his paper. Although nothing of the sort ever occurred to me, it clearly exacerbated the Manuscripts fracas. The negotiations our Realist group entered into with the Old Czechs had mainly to do with the press: we wanted to influence it, improve it. The Old Czech journalists opposed us of course. Then in 1887 the journal *Čas* (Time) — which, as I've said, I didn't even know about — brought out that unfortunate Schauer article in the first issue. Our group wanted to start a journal of its own, but the young people wanted one too and got to it before we did. When my enemies ascribed the article to me and people started arguing over it, I answered the charges in *Čas* and from that time on wrote regularly for it. Later I switched to *Naše doba* (Our Times).

In 1900 *Čas* became a daily, and I became a regular at the editorial office, though doing more advising than writing. The most pleasant memory I have of my work there dates from 1914, the beginning of the war, when a group of us — Dr. Herben, Pfeffermann the engineer, Kunte, myself, and later Beneš* — would meet to go over the military situation. Those meetings gave rise to top-notch articles — insofar as the censor let them through. I myself wrote two articles for *Naše doba* assessing the strengths of the opposing camps. I was afraid that a short war would fail to liberate us even if Austria were defeated: we weren't ready, and the warring powers were all but ignorant of us. So I gave a great deal of thought to how long it would last. Much as I feared a short war, I reproached myself for being so cruel as to wish it long.

There's so much I could tell you about newspapers! The fact that I get so angry at them every day goes to show how much they mean to me. We have had two great journalists: Havlíček and Neruda (though Neruda was not so much a journalist as a columnist and cultural commentator); both had all the marks of the trade. Journalists must be well educated and clever; they must be keen observers and keen judges; they must be indifferent to nothing, because the whole world, the whole of day-to-day existence, is their canvas. Being a journalist means studying and understanding contemporary society. I say "studying and understanding" because the journalist who judges everything by the standards of his political party is nothing more than a preacher or a squabbler. The lowly reporter who gives an accurate account of events does a more important, more honest job. And of course a good journalist must have character and exercise freedom of speech. Freedom, freedom! . . .

*

In 1905-06 the issue of universal suffrage came to the fore. The Emperor and Beck hoped that the entry into Parliament of parties dealing with social issues would weaken national strife; the Czech parties backed it because it could only win votes.

The first elections based on universal suffrage took place in 1907. A progressive political association in Moravian Walachia led by some disciples of mine came up with the idea of drafting me as a candidate. (I think Professor Dědina put me forward, but it was the late Dr. Kraicz who informed me about it.) And so I came to be the candidate for Moravian Walachia (which also happened to be the region with the greatest number of *Naše doba* subscribers). My opponent, Povondra, belonged to the Clerical Party, and was backed largely by the clergy, who campaigned against me by telling the poor Walachians I was out to destroy the family. There was at the time a campaign for the legalization of divorce, and even though I had nothing to do with it my opponents ascribed it to me. I would go to the rallies with a Bible in my pocket, and when some priest or parson defended the indissolubility of marriage I would read a passage from the Gospel of Saint Matthew proving that Jesus condoned divorce. So much for the reverend gentleman. I was disgusted with the way politicians reiterated catchwords. I preferred to speak on alcoholism or the economic situation — things like that — so people would have something concrete to think about. Anyway, I won the election and went back to Vienna. There were two of us Realists there: Professor Drtina and I.

Why did the Clerical Party turn against me? When I first arrived in Prague as a professor, even the Catholics gave me a decent reception: Father Vychodil wrote a highly appreciative review of my work on Pascal, for example. But later they dug out a passage from *Suicide* where I say that Catholicism is impossible for us, which didn't seem to prevent German Catholics in the Empire from referring to the book with admiration (Ratzinger). But that's the point: German Catholics were better educated. I believe I criticized the philosophical works of Czech Catholics in *Athenaeum*. Well, they *were* weak. Later, during the Manuscripts Controversy, it was the Catholic daily *Čech* (The Czech) that came down on me the hardest, and during the Hilsner affair it was the Catholic papers that called the tune against me. They were the ones that accused me of corrupting the young and so on. They couldn't forgive me for making so much of the Czech Reformation and placing our native Czech tradition over an ancient but fictitious Slav culture. The reason I make so much of our Reformation is that it was primarily a moral, religious movement rather than a theological one. What mattered most to Hus — and to Štítný before him — was moral reform. In their writings I found what had perplexed me as a child when I observed the strange lives priests lived. My break with the Catholic Church was a matter of morals, not of dogma — Protestants, after all, have the same basic dogmas — though I had to break with dogmas too when they failed to pass the test of reason. That holds for dogmas of all religions, of course. What I cannot accept by reason I cannot accept by faith. I hope to have my final say on the matter some time soon.

Nor did I then — as I do not now — care for liberalism, at least insofar as it implies religious indifference and superficiality. Catholicism — particularly in Austria, where it was the official faith, protected by both the police and the bureaucracy — actually promoted this moral laxity. (I have always maintained that Jesus needs no police.) It goes without saying that in Austria fighting the state meant fighting the state church. In fact, it was the alliance of the sword and the censer that made our religious life so ineffectual. The Czech Reformation was fundamentally an anti-Austrian movement, which is something our liberals do not grasp to this day.

In the course of my skirmishes with the clergy I had a public debate at Hradec Králové with Fathers Reyl and Jemelka. It was a sign of progress that such a discussion was even possible. A large number of seminarians and young priests would ask me to advise them whether to leave the Church because of one or another scruple. I usually advised them against it, feeling their doubts were not strong enough to lead them to another positive faith. One young chaplain admitted to me that the only thing about his office that held his interest was confessing women and girls. I did not advocate leaving the Church so long as the doubts stemmed from indifference, politics (like the Los-von-Rom-Bewegung, the

Break with Rome movement), or a desire to marry. I wanted people to be honest about their religious feelings.

Another conflict I had at the time was the catechist trial. At one rally or other I happened to mention the case of a catechist who had denounced his fellow teachers. Somehow things got distorted, and three hundred and eight catechists charged me with having accused all catechists of spying and writing denunciations. I won my case. Here too the issue was mutual assistance between Church and state, the state protecting the Church and the Church serving the state as a kind of spiritual police free of charge. Today Catholics should be able to see that it helped neither the Church nor our Czech Catholicism.

Then there was the Wahrmund affair. Wahrmund, a professor of ecclesiastical law at Innsbruck, wrote a pamphlet criticizing the Church. It was confiscated, and Wahrmund landed in hot water. Lueger, the leader of the Viennese Clerical Party, stood up in Parliament and asked how a man like that could be a university professor. In other words, it was a matter of academic and scholarly freedom. I opposed Lueger. There was a big hue and cry over it, but all the progressive parties, including the Germans, backed me. Even conservatives like the Poles allowed that Lueger had overstepped the mark. The quarrel attracted attention abroad as well. If we Czechs want to earn our place in the world, we must make questions of interest to the world our own questions and formulate our own responses to them, but we must also make our "Czech question" a question of interest to the world. We managed to do so for the first time during the war.

*

While we're on the subject of the Church, let me say that I consider neither the Church nor theology to be religion, or at least not the whole of religion. We intellectuals like to sink our teeth into the teachings and theory of this or that Church, but that's not religion. I refuse to think of religion in the abstract. I can still picture Sunday mornings in Čejkovice: the whole community coming together, friends greeting one another, boys meeting girls, all in their Sunday best; incense burning, music playing, the entire village singing, everyone standing and kneeling at the same time, squire and groom; the drama at the altar, the sermon you understand and the ritualistic Latin you do not. Think what those Sundays give to people, how they bind them together into a like-minded collective. The Catholic Mass is, as it were, a folk festival; Protestantism has fewer ceremonious rituals and enters more into everyday life. Churches influence life by dividing up and framing the year in terms of religion. Thus we have Sundays and holidays, which are *de facto* the continuation of pagan and nature-related festivals. The Church presides over a person's entire life: birth, maturation, marriage, and death — it is all ordained and highly systematized. You must remember that people in a small village like mine had nothing else. It made a very strong bond. The rites of the Church, like other rituals, came about at a time when people did not read as they do today, when they were an unlettered mass — a situation that lasted until the nineteenth century! Nowadays they read, they have plays, concerts, and lectures to go to, they have films and radio for the eyes and ears, they have clubs, teams, and political parties to draw them together. And instead of the divine service they have a fat Sunday paper. I wonder as I thumb through it, "Can this really take the place of the services I knew as a child?"

Of course, the advance of history alters the Church's mission. The Church actually took over the Roman Empire and preserved part of the culture of antiquity; it had a thousand-year monopoly on schools and schooling; it reserved all humanitarian services — hospitals, poorhouses — for itself; it sustained a kind of Pan-Europe among the various nations and potentates, even a kind of world unity. To do so it worked out a vast international, universal program of organization. Today the tasks it once undertook have passed into other hands, the hands of the state. The Church has been unable to maintain its schools, it has ceased to cultivate and oversee scholarship, even humanitarian services have been taken over by social legislation, and international and cultural relations are entirely in lay hands: for better or for worse, economic interests now hold the world together. By putting all this in terms of the formula that theocracy is giving way to democracy, I do not mean that religion is losing its importance or mission. The Church must continue to care for the soul and attend to practical morality. If that were what priests did, they would be closer to Jesus. Nearly every family has its moral problems;

141

recognizing them and restoring the soul sinking beneath them should be the duty of all priests. But then they need a knowledge of humanity, they need deep inner resources. Where are we to find men like that?

There is no stopping it: the world is becoming progressively more worldly, state-oriented; the Church is no longer the political and social force it once was. Besides, modern criticism and science are eating away at all dogmas and theologies. Hence the crisis in Churches of all denominations.

Yet the task of Christianity — the task of all Churches — is as great as (if not greater than) it has been these two thousand years: its task is to become the true herald of practical love and reviver of souls. How to go about it is for the Churches themselves to say. Religion, now and in future, will be more individual; it will tend to personal, spiritual needs. I am not a prophet, but I see myself as one of those future believers. What we need is freedom of scholarship and research, intellectual integrity in matters of religion, tolerance; not spiritual indifference, no, but faith, living faith in something higher than ourselves, something great, sublime, and eternal.

My squabbles with the historians? Oh well, if I must. Among other things I consider myself a philosopher of history. While still at the Gymnasium, I wondered whether schoolboys a million years hence would still be reciting the names and dates of the French kings and their wars. There is no such thing as history per se; there is only the history of something, that is, the history of mathematics, philosophy, art, and so on, or hats and shoes, if you like, or of knowledge as a whole, or of the universe. It is always something changing and evolving. Not movement itself, something moving. So I've always wanted historians to tell me what they're writing the history of. If it's the history of the state, then what is a state and how did today's state grow out of its past origins?

To continue: I am not against history; I am against historicism. By that I mean that the past is no argument in and of itself: the past contains both good and evil. I will invoke only what is good in the past. And in the present and "modernity." Both oppressor and oppressed can invoke history. What has been, the mere fact that it has been, is a comfortable argument for the reactionary. What interests me is how the good and evil that were yesterday and are today — how they came about. History may be the *magistra vitae*, the teacher of life, but how many we have had and which among them have been true teachers?

*

The Zagreb trial and the Friedjung trial that followed gave me a taste of diplomacy. They brought me into the campaign against Aehrenthal, the Austrian Minister for Foreign Affairs, and into foreign politics. Here is how it happened. In 1909 the Hungarians brought fifty-three Croat intellectuals and peasants to trial on a trumped-up charge of high treason. Their lives were at stake. Now I had contacts in Bosnia and Croatia from the time of my campaign against Kállay; I also had a number of pupils there. They came to me and begged me to go to Zagreb. I can't say I was keen to go: I was afraid it would take too much time. But, well, in the end I went, attended the trial, and brought the case up in Parliament. The sentence was reversed.

The second trial was the Friedjung case. Friedjung, a professor of history at the University of Vienna, had published a forged document meant to substantiate a Serb plot against Austria. I could tell at first glance it was a forgery; after all, I knew people in Serbia and Croatia and knew their intentions and activities. Supilo, a Croat member of Parliament, assured me he had proof that the forgery had been perpetrated by agents of the Minister of Foreign Affairs and an envoy by the name of Forgách. That wasn't enough for me — I wanted to get all the details and get them on the spot — so I went to Belgrade several times and even found the holes in the door they pinned the document to while photographing it. I also had a good look at Vasić, who put together the document.

The friends I made then in Serbia and Croatia stood me in good stead during the war. In the course of both trials I also got to know Wickham Steed, the Vienna-based *London Times* correspondent for the Balkans and Central Europe. That opened the columns of the *Times* to us during the war.

*

In 1910 I celebrated my sixtieth birthday, and there was a banquet and speeches. Apparently I responded by saying that everything I'd done till then was mere preparation and that my real work lay ahead. Some later regarded that remark as a prophecy of what I was to do during the war. Well, I'm no prophet! I didn't know how to respond to the speeches, that's all. All I meant was that I had more work to do. . .

The Pre-War Years

The years immediately preceding the war I spent in Parliament. I also did some writing and brought out *Russia and Europe*. A German publisher by the name of Diederichs had read my Tolstoy obituary and commissioned me to collect everything I'd done on Russia for publication. Two parts have appeared so far; the third, on Dostoevsky, is still in manuscript. There are so many things I'd like to write about, but the time! Where am I to find the time?

I was re-elected to Parliament in 1911; Professor Drtina was not. I made common cause with Prunar and Kalina of the Constitutional Party and the Moravian Progressives Stránský, Sr. and Votruba.

The Šviha affair! It showed how unprepared we were for things to come. Imagine charging a Czech member of Parliament with being paid like a common police spy. What they must have thought of us! I was convinced that Šviha was not the same person as Wiener the police informer, though Šviha did side with the heir to the throne and supply him with information. Šviha was in debt and was promised remuneration for his services, but because the heir to the throne was such a skinflint, he had the police pay Šviha. At least that was how I saw it. Politically it was more of a crime than if Šviha *had* been in the pay of the police, but from the human standpoint it was more tolerable. I took an active part in the trial: I wanted Šviha to be tried *in camera caritatis*, as, say, Sabina had been. I had no way of knowing at the time that my part in the Šviha affair would offend certain people to such an extent that it rankled even after the war broke out.

144

On the other hand, it's true — and I willingly admit it — that in this and other instances I made mistakes. Though I must also say that I always got my comeuppance.

*

It's strange all the issues and disputes I've been involved in, often against my will. I used to think I was wasting my time with so many interests. Not until the war did I realize that everything or nearly everything that I'd done or that had come my way had been good for something. It was good — and useful during the war — that I'd been born half Slovak and lived and worked among Slovaks: I was able to talk to them and on their behalf as one of them. It was good I'd studied in Vienna and was known there: as a member of Parliament I had kept close tabs on the Viennese court, the military bigwigs, the nobility, and the higher ranks of the bureaucracy, and all this knowledge came in handy during the war, when I needed to demonstrate Austria's moral degeneration and inevitable downfall.

My conflicts and skirmishes — over the Manuscripts, constitutional rights, or the meaning of our history — also led me beyond politics to the study of national issues. I would never have become a politician had I not been forced to experience the historical problems of our nation so acutely. My battles brought me into contact with all strata of our people; my debates taught me diplomacy. For there is such a thing as literary and journalistic diplomacy, and I needed it and used it throughout the war.

Ever since childhood my head has spinned with Slav issues: first the Polish question, later Russian problems. Everything I'd read and thought about Russia brought me closer to the Russians and gave me credence among them. I knew what we could and could not expect of the people. I was familiar with the atmosphere in which our own revolutionary army took shape. Had I not known Russia so intimately I might well have failed to find my bearings in the chaos of the Russian Revolution. I've always been on friendly terms with the Poles. As a member of Parliament I championed the South Slav cause in Bosnia, in the Zagreb trial, and in the Friedjung affair, which won us the cooperation of the South Slavs

145

during the war. The Friedjung affair required a bit of detective work on my part, and that too proved invaluable in wartime. My quarrel with Aehrenthal taught me a great deal about official diplomacy and brought me in touch with Wickham Steed and Seton-Watson. It also made me known in England, France, and elsewhere.

The fact that my wife was American opened the Anglo-Saxon world to me, and the fact that I knew its language and culture greatly facilitated my work in England and America during the war. My knowledge of languages has been very useful in general: I have been able to speak and lecture in Russia, France, England, and America. I can get along in Italian as well. The lectures I gave in America helped me to meet people of great service to us in the war.

Not until the war did I reap the benefits of the Hilsner case. As I've pointed out, Jews exercised a great influence on newspapers in all the Allied countries, and wherever I went the papers were for us or at least not against us. You have no idea what that meant.

I have had many such experiences. I believe in teleology, that is, I believe that each of us is led by Providence, though how I cannot say.

*

Yes, I'm a realist, as I've been told, but I have romantic tendencies as well. I see no contradiction in that. I am personally closest to the romantic poets: Mácha, Pushkin, Musset, Byron.

I continually have to hold myself in check. When I chose realism and the scientific method, I had to restrain my own romanticism, impose a certain mental discipline on myself. I make an attempt to be a realist in practice, a conscious and constant attempt. Just as I overcame my Slav anarchy by means of Anglo-Saxon models, I overcame the Plato in me with Locke, Hume, and the other empiricists. People don't seem to understand that criticism, especially harsh criticism, is often a matter of self-criticism and even painful confession. I also have an inner conflict between the impulsive Slovak and the sober Czech. Humans are not simple creatures. I have often suffered when adversaries and followers alike wish to make me into a one-sided type.

Take my notorious rationalism, for instance. If I'm going to teach and make my points, then I've got to use reason and reasonable arguments, haven't I? But always and in everything, in scholarship and in politics, my motivating force, my *vis motrix*, has been ethical in nature, and ethics I base on feelings, love, sympathy, and humanity. If I was once a one-sided rationalist, it was due to a fault in my philosophical education. Circumstances have often forced me to criticize both the right and the left, but my criticism never stemmed from rationalism, or certainly not from rationalism alone. Logic and feeling are not mutually exclusive.

Politics has an element of poetry to it, inasmuch as it has creative power. I believe we can consciously fashion, mold our own lives and those of our dear ones to a considerable extent; I believe a life can and must be created; I believe life itself is a play just as a Shakespeare play is life itself. And what is politics — true politics — but the conscious formation of people, the fashioning and molding of real life?

Politics too calls for a balance between reason and emotion. Even in the most heated political situation we must be observant and plan how to go about things and what we can count on. We must be as precise as mathematicians. We must not allow our feelings to err in their observations and appraisals. The aim, the ideal, is established by feelings as much as reason. And while the means are dictated by reason, we can change the situation to suit our aim, introducing new elements, elements of our own. Such is creation; such is the poetry of life.

The war years were of course the most romantic period in my life, though even then I stuck to the straight and narrow, the rational. By romantic I don't mean only the romance of war and conspiracy. How unprepared we were going into it, yet in fact we were merely putting the finishing touches on a century of efforts by men like Dobrovský, Kollár, Palacký, and Havlíček; how isolated we were — the people at home as well as those of us abroad — yet how deftly we carried out the mandate of the nation, setting out with our bare hands and bringing back freedom, the Republic, Slovakia, Ruthenia — it still seems a dream to me. Now there's a case of Providence for you.

What I'm saying is, your method must be absolutely practical,

sensible, realistic, but your goal — the conception, the whole — is a never-ending poem. Goethe had a phrase for it: *exakte Phantasie.*

*

Oh, the romance of life! Long, long ago, as I've told you, I thought of writing a Czech novel crammed with the romance of my life. I began it while at school and made several attempts thereafter, quite serious attempts after my experience in Prague. It was meant to be autobiographical, *Dichtung und Wahrheit*, a combination of poetry and reality, but when I saw I wasn't getting anywhere I gave up on it and burned everything I'd written. I realized I lacked the necessary artistry, and I didn't want it to be another lecture from the podium. My life has been full; I've seen a lot. I've begun to forget the details and exact chronological order, but even my forgetting has a method to it: everything over and done with I simply toss out of my head so as to leave it free and tidy; it's like clearing off a desk. Yet to be frank, I can't say everything, and not only out of consideration for others: I doubt one ever has words adequate to one's innermost feelings. A good reader will find me between the lines of my books.

THE WAR

The Early Years

The outbreak of the war found me on holiday in the Saxon town of Schandau. When the heir to the throne was assassinated in Sarajevo, I both expected and did not expect things to proceed as they did. I expected something because for years I had felt "something in the air"; I expected nothing because I knew the Serb government had had no hand in it. I knew many people in Serbia, and I knew their plans. True, there was agtitation aimed at Austria-Hungary in Bosnia Herzegovina and in Croatia as well, but the Serb government was not involved. No, it wanted a pact with Austria; Pašić had made perfectly acceptable overtures to Minister Berchtold through me. There was good will on the Serb side. I also know that (official) Serbia was moderate during the war.

Once mobilization began I was unable to leave Germany, there being no connections, so I observed the mobilization process, going all the way to Dresden and other towns for the purpose. I must say I was impressed. Everything was serious and orderly, everything ready to the last detail. I never saw an inebriated German, while whole trainloads of Austrian recruits on their way home for duty were soused. I realize they drank out of desperation, but it does reflect on the state.

I hoped Germany would be defeated, but knew it would take much doing and be harder than anybody imagined. Austria, on the other hand, would soon be at the end of her tether, her moral tether primarily. I feared for France: she was likely to be taken unawares by a swift German onrush. But it was Russia I was most concerned about. My last visit there, in 1910, had been to see the army more than to see Tolstoy, and what I saw was disorder and a lack of preparation. Things had improved slightly after the Russo-Japanese War, but not much. I knew the representative of the Russian Telegraph Agency in Vienna,

Svatkovsky, and he came to see me either at the beginning of the hostilities or shortly after Sarajevo. He spoke of Russia with great apprehension and opposed the plan, current at the time, of handing over Bohemia to a Russian Grand Duke. "You wouldn't put up with the rule of the best of Russian Grand Dukes in Prague," he told me, "not for a fortnight." I didn't expect much of Tsarist Russia either militarily or morally. I based my belief that Germany would lose the war on numerical comparisons between the economic and human resources of both sides. It never occurred to me that America might help.

Back in Prague I observed that our men were loath to report for duty; they behaved as though being sent to the slaughterhouse. There was resistance, and people were arrested. Yet only someone with no inkling of conditions in Bohemia could have expected an uprising. When I decided I had to take action against Austria, I did not tell myself I was a patriot and my country needed me; I simply had a bad conscience at the thought that our men were going to war or to jail while we members of Parliament stayed at home. What I did tell myself was, "You're in Parliament. Do something!" Of course I thought about what could happen to me and my family, but that's par for the course.

The first thing I did was go to Holland. My passport was valid for all countries in Europe, and I obtained a visa to accompany my sister-in-law to the boat — she was returning to America. You know her. Esperanza. (It now occurs to me her name means hope.) I then got another visa and went back. Holland was a good place to gather information and make contact with my English friends Wickham Steed and Seton-Watson. Seton-Watson came over just to see me. I spoke to him for two whole days, outlining our problems and the need to break up Austria and transform Central Europe. He used what I said to compose a memorandum for Lord Grey, which the Russians and certain others also received.

Then, in December, I went to Italy. I was on pins and needles at home, and I wanted to talk things over with my Serb and Croat friends. The excuse I gave was that I needed to take my daughter Olga to the south. At the Italian frontier the stationmaster tried to stop us by saying he had to telegraph to Prague for permission to let us proceed. For the first time in my life I threw my weight around, telling him I was a member of Parliament and I'd make it hot for him if he held us back. All he did was shrug his shoulders. There we stood on the platform, the train starting to move in the direction of Italy. What were we to do? We jumped aboard, and off we went. We had purposely brought next to no luggage; if we hadn't, we might not have made it across the border.

At the time I expected to be back in Prague within a few weeks; I didn't return for four years after crossing the border, four years to the day. I had only the several thousand Beneš had given me; *de facto* Beneš financed the initial stage of our revolution. I had arranged with Scheiner for some funding from the Sokols, and he gave me reason to hope for support from our fellow countrymen in America, but not much was forthcoming as long as the United States remained neutral. We didn't know how to handle these things. No one but Scheiner even thought of the need for money, though before leaving Prague I'd charged Voska, who was there at the time, to raise money in America for the imprisoned and the families of men who had been put to death. In any case, we were short on funds throughout the war. I don't think the world has ever seen such a cheap revolution.

In Venice I met the editor Hlaváč, who gave me the latest from Vienna. From there I went on to Florence, then to Rome. I stayed near Monte Pincio. I was glad to see ancient Rome again, but spent most of my time renewing old ties and seeking new ones. I had no set plan in mind, of course; I'd set out from Prague empty-handed, into the void. I found plenty of Serbs, Croats, and Slovenes, but they were not united: they represented various movements, such as Great Serb, Great Croat, and Yugoslav. I saw a lot of Supilo and Vošjak. The Italian "Dalmazia nostra" campaign was already underway. One of the people I visited, Professor Lumbroso the historian, clasped his hands when he saw me: there had been stories in the papers of massacres in Prague and I had been reported shot. He showed me a file of clippings about me — *morto!* I got to know the British ambassador and informed him of conditions in Austria; he in turn passed on some letters to Wickham Steed for me. I went to see him at night, and still I was tailed by Austrian and German spies — he warned me to be on my guard. Svatkovsky came all the way to Rome to meet me and passed my report on to Russia. I visited the Russian Legation regularly. I had to convince everyone of the necessity for the break-up of Austria-Hungary, the general belief at the time being that a Danube monarchy should be retained as a rampart between Germany and the Balkans. I constantly discussed the issue, eager to get home as soon as possible. I hid my books with their marginal notes and especially a sheaf of papers containing inside information on the Habsburg dynasty I'd accumulated during my term in Parliament. I was afraid they'd put my wife in jail if they found it. It never crossed my mind they'd take it out on my daughter Alice. I saw that sheaf of papers before me day and night. Of course both it and the books were eventually confiscated. And lost.

I remained in Rome a month or so. From there I drove with an Italian diplomat to Genoa and from Genoa on to Geneva. In Geneva I was to meet Ernest Denis and then return home. But even the Austrian consul advised me against it. He himself brought up the war and ventured the opinion that Austria would lose. Soon I got two messages — one from Beneš in Prague, telling me not to come home because I'd be arrested at the border, and one from Machar in Vienna, telling me I'd be hanged at the border. So I stayed.

It was strange. I was like a wound-up machine. I could think of nothing but our campaign against Austria; I saw nothing else, felt nothing else, I was hypnotized by it. The only thing I cared about was the war — what the day-to-day situation was, how things were going at the front — and whom to speak to next, how to reach people and arouse their interest. I would rack my brains trying to outwit the border guards and get news to and from Prague. I forgot what it meant to sleep; I could count on my fingers how many decent nights of sleep I had during those four years.

There were several of our people in Geneva: Dr. Sychrava, then Božinov, an engineer by the name of Baráček, who designed an encoder for us, a handful of students, a Czech workmen's society, and later Dürich, a member of Parliament. We had direct communication with Paris because Kepl made regular trips there. By then Štefánik had begun his propaganda in the various salons and associations of Paris. He had a true gift for social proselytizing, for inspiring people; he won us much affection and interest. Twice Beneš came with news from Prague. Svatkovsky came too. I had talks with Denis and Professor Eisenmann, who was with the French Ministry of War at the time. The Serb general consul gave me a Serb passport, but I used my own name, birthplace, and profession because I did not want to tell needless lies or have to worry about giving myself away. I was simply registered as a Serb citizen. I went to Lyon to have a look at the French recruits. I'd heard they were revolting and wanted to see for myself. I managed to get into the barracks and found the soldiers in high spirits and perfectly reliable. Then I went to Paris to see Denis and talk over the publication of *La Nation tchèque*. Štefánik had just had an operation, and I visited him daily at the hospital. He was very sentimental; he called me "little father" and kept trying to pat and kiss me. The difference in our ages prevented me from feeling as close to him as he felt to me. I had known him when he was a student in Prague. I remember his coming to see me once, frozen stiff. He had no overcoat so I gave him mine. I had to get it altered for him too: it was too big. That was fairly typical. You must recall that nearly all our leading personalities came from poverty-stricken backgrounds and had bouts with hunger. Well, the hungry eat the full, as the saying goes.

I stayed at the Hotel Richmond in Geneva and went back and forth to Annemasse in France when we had trouble printing our paper in Switzerland. I even thought of going to Serbia and learned to ride so I could follow the cavalry. I kept studying the war and everything connected with it. Although I'd arrived in Geneva with hardly a sheet of paper, I built up another library and put together my "dovecote," a set of shelves with cubbyholes for reviews, newspaper clippings, and notes. When I moved to London in 1915, I took several crates of books and papers with me, all of them dealing with the war and politics. My only relaxation was taking walks around the lake and reading French novels. I was able to catch up on French literature, which I had neglected for some years.

Sending messengers to Prague required a great deal of time and energy. I didn't want to use the usual tricks — like sewing a report into a collar or inserting it in the heel of a shoe — because the Austrian officials were obviously on to them. The technical problems involved were sometimes quite complex: sliding a slip of paper under the regulator of a watch, sinking the right kind of hole in an umbrella, slipping a rolled-up letter into a pencil from which a piece of lead had been extracted. It was mostly Baráček the engineer who performed these feats for us. A Czech cabinetmaker designed some suitcases with double sides rather than double bottoms, the trick being to make it sound solid when knocked. Well, he did it. Another time we put reports in oil barrels and had to find an unobtrusive way to mark them. There were times we failed. Once a messenger had a report bound inside the covers of a Smetana opera, but he panicked during the customs inspection on the train. Luckily he found a way to throw it out of the window.

Finding messengers and preparing them psychologically was even harder. They were of all types: some educated, others quite simple, both men and women. I interviewed each of them personally, giving them an idea of what might happen to them on the way and what might make things hot for them in Prague and giving them tips on how to handle themselves. The psychological and technical gymnastics involved! Somersaults even. Of course the messengers had to buy their tickets outside of Geneva, Geneva being suspect.

We also had to keep an eye out for Austrian spies. One did show up, but Prague sent us word about him in time. He was a photographer for our picture magazines. I recognized him the moment he arrived, and sent him on to our people, who took him in and managed to learn something about what was going on at home from him.

Then there was the curious case of D., an Austrian officer of Moravian extraction. He came to see me at the Hotel Richmond with an outlandish story about the Viennese court and the archdukes. If I remember correctly, there was even a murder in it. He may have concocted it to win me over, but because it was so typical of Vienna I published it as a *feuilleton* in the *Neue Zürcher Zeitung*, I believe. I also wanted to test him, and I saw he didn't like it at all. I went to Zurich to look into his supposed contacts with a group of Englishman. I couldn't locate them. He was very eager to get to Paris: he claimed to have invented a device for improving the aim of bombs dropped from aircraft, and he wanted to turn it over to the Allies. I got him a residency permit for Annemasse, on French soil, where Dr. Sychrava was living and working, and sent the plans for his device to Paris. Paris wrote back that they had hundreds and hundreds of such plans and were not interested in his.

Whereupon Mr. D. vanished. So I imagine that he too was a spy and that since he got nothing out of us he used us to cross into France. When we went for walks in the outskirts of Annemasse, I always carried a loaded gun, kept an eye on him, and wouldn't let him get behind me.

There is no revolution or war without deceit and lies. It would be naive to see only heroism in them: Achilles would have been impossible without Odysseus. That is why a society without wars and revolution would be on a morally higher plane. I made it a rule to lie as little as I could. No matter how cautious you are, you get caught: you forget the details you invent and end by giving yourself away. I worked out my own method: when sending off our messengers, I was careful to find out everything about their circumstances and aptitudes so as to provide the procedural instructions best suited to them and thus avoid unnecessary ruses. It's strange how people enjoy lying to one another and that, aware of it though they are, they go on believing one another. Lying is the handmaiden of violence, so lies, even as a protective measure, must be used as sparingly as possible. I have learned through practice that in battle too the straight road is the shortest.

I can also tell you that in war as in politics (war being the hand-maiden of politics) psychology is of the essence. I was lucky enough to be well acquainted with our people at home, so I knew ahead of time who would play what kind of role in this drama of ours. I was familiar with enough strata of Vienna — the court, the bureaucracy, the press — to predict or deduce from hints what the overall situation was like. I had to study the characters of our collaborators and our secret adversaries both. Before I went to see anyone important, I would get hold of his biography to learn how best to approach him. Academic psychology was of no help whatever, of course; only life and — novels. For seventy years now I've been reading novels daily; not until recently have I left out a day now and then to give my eyes a rest. I live in literature, I couldn't exist without it: it contains so much experience, such knowledge of the human spirit. I think I have good insight into people, though I do misjudge them every once in a while. A human is a devilishly involved and perplexing machine. And each one so different!

*

When Beneš showed up — and it was high time, because he would have been caught and arrested had he stayed any longer in Prague — I was very happy; when he showed me the passport he'd used to cross the German border (he had crossed the Austrian border in secret), I nearly lost my temper. How could he have dared to arrive at the border with such a poorly done passport! Ridiculous as it seems, I felt both anger and delight at the thought of the German officials letting him through with that excuse for a document. Beneš made things a bit easier on me: I had comparatively few contacts in France, whereas Beneš had studied in Paris and was at home there. Fortune thus determined our division of labor: he worked in Paris, I elsewhere.

I first met Beneš as a colleague at the University. Early in the war he joined us at *Čas* (Time) as a volunteer, saying he wanted to learn the trade. I saw at once he was the practical type. Once he was on his way to see me (I was living opposite the Chotek Gardens at the time) when we met in the street and walked to the *Čas* office together. He said his conscience had been bothering him and we needed to take action. I told him I had. I'd just come back from my first trip to Holland. As we walked, I outlined everything I'd done and what I had in mind. I remember coming down the hill from Letná and seeing all Prague spread out before us and thinking of Queen Libuše's prophecy: "I see a city whose glory shall reach the stars." But our first concern was money. He promised at once he would raise some. And he did.

In Switzerland I got to know him better, and let me tell you: were it not for Beneš there would be no Czecho-slovak Republic. The two of us saw eye to eye on the main issues. Even when I was away, the decisions Beneš made tallied completely with the overall approach we had agreed upon. Once, later on in the war, he came from Paris to London to see me, and after he reported on what he was doing, how things were going, and how our cause was gradually coming into its own, I said to him, "Beneš, you and I are going to be friends."

*

In 1915, on the five hundredth anniversary of the burning of Jan Hus at the stake, I appeared with Ernest Denis at a public demonstration against

Austria chaired by Lucien Gautier at Reformation Hall in Geneva. I chose the day to remind the world of the historical continuity involved and of the history of our state in general. By then I knew that either we won or I would never go back to Austria.

While I was in Geneva, my son Herbert died: he had caught typhus from Galician refugees. Then my daughter Alice was imprisoned in connection with the button affair. A certain Czech living in Geneva, a Social Democrat, upset that his Party at home in Bohemia was not working hard enough against Austria, took it upon himself to send a messenger, a woman, with a secret letter concealed in a red button. All she had to do was deliver the button to Dr. Soukup. Well, the woman got to Prague with no mishap and had her father-in-law, a workman, deliver the button. Now our people must have been suspicious of him, thinking him an *agent provocateur*, and the long and the short of it was that the button fell into the hands of the police, and the usual round of arrests began. When Alice was arrested, the women of America presented a petition to the Austrian government. I learned by hearsay that my wife had fallen ill, and I was afraid Alice would not be able to stand imprisonment. The American papers reported that my son Jan, who was in the army, had been or was going to be hanged on account of me. All this and much else unnerved me, of course, but it did not break me. I lived in a dream: all I could see was our goal. When friends tried to comfort me, I put on a heroic front, as if it were nothing. It's par for the course, I would say.

A person can put up with a great deal, everything, in fact, if he has a goal and vows to follow it truthfully, come what may. Truthfulness is the secret of the world and of life; it is a sacrament religious and moral.

London

I traveled from Geneva to London for the first time in April 1915 to see Wickham Steed, Seton-Watson, Sarolea, and a few others. There I composed a memorandum for the British government and the other Allies. I'd been warned to expect a spy in the sleeping car from Geneva to Paris. Very well, I thought, as long as I know who I'm traveling with. So I altered neither the day of my departure nor the number of my compartment; I simply put my briefcase under my pillow and rode on.

I moved my headquarters to London at the end of September. Beneš and Štefánik were taking care of Paris, where Allied policy was basically decided. England had more weight in economic affairs.

It was natural that I should have known the Anglo-Saxons better than any other nation; it came from my having married an American. But I learned French before I learned English, and I read so much French and got to know France so well through what I read that I never went to Paris before the war, preferring, as I've said, to visit countries and cultures I knew less well. The only time I'd spent in France was in French ports and their environs on my way to and from America.

I've always liked being in London. In a large city like that you can be alone even in the midst of millions of people. The first place I lived during the war was Miss Brown's boarding house at 4 Holford Road, Hampstead. I would ride into town on the top of a bus, watching the swarms of people and traffic. I didn't like using a car. Why pay more, I said to myself, when you can get there on so little? Our people said a person in my position ought to have his own car, but in town I'd have my meals at a Lyons (it was cheap: you could get a decent meal for ten or fifteen pence), and only when I had guests and had to think of my position would I go to the Café Royal.

I suffered a lot from the cold at the boarding house — those English fireplaces don't give off much heat — and in the autumn of 1916 Olga found a small furnished house belonging to a Pastor Wilder who'd been recalled to America. It too was in Hampstead, 21 Platt's Lane. It came with everything you can imagine, including a cook, so I started eating at home. I would take walks on Hampstead Heath, sometimes even at night when I was anxious, when there was talk of a separate peace with Austria, for instance. Once I gashed my head colliding with a lamp post in the London fog. Sirens would periodically go off to warn us of German air raids, and we were all supposed to take cover in basements or tunnels, though I much preferred standing in the garden and looking on. Once we saw two burning Zeppelins over Hendon, another time — thirty-six planes amidst a veritable downpour of shells. What a sight! I was constantly finding shrapnel in the garden. A German submarine bombarded Brighton when I was there.

Once a band of burglars tried to break into the house. The police thought they were after my papers and advised me to install alarms on all the doors and windows and the fireplace. In Switzerland I had had a curious rash on my shoulders and the doctor thought it was from poison; in England it came back on my neck, and they lanced it and sent me to Bournemouth, to the sea, to recover. The English doctors too said it was poisoning that came from my linen and was perhaps the doing of my political adversaries. I thought it was lack of fresh air, and so later when I was in America I started riding again. They say you breathe in twice as much air when you ride as when you walk. I also had influenza several times.

People can put up with all kinds of things. I was aware a spy or fanatic could try to assassinate me, but I wasn't at all afraid. When Beneš came to see me, I told him that if I were murdered he should make use of my death for propaganda purposes. I even drew up a kind of will, a sorry affair, as I had nothing to leave but a few writings — and debts.

In London I had a bit of passport trouble. You'll remember I was given a Serb passport in Geneva, but to keep from contradicting myself if I were interrogated I filled in everything but "nationality" according to the truth: place of birth — Hodonín, Moravia; profession — university professor, etc. Nobody batted an eye until I went to take out some money from the London branch of the Swiss bank where I had my account. The bank clerk shook his head when he saw it — he was Swiss German and well enough acquainted with the geography of the region to know that Moravia wasn't in Serbia — but I took him down a peg. "Since you're so well up on geography," I said, "you ought to know that the Morava is a river in Serbia, though what is my passport to you anyway?" Still, I switched my account to another bank.

For a long time I was followed around Hampstead by a detective. It must have been the passport again. By then I'd been appointed professor at the University of London, King's College (I wasn't particularly eager to teach, but it was a good thing for me to hold the position), and Asquith, the Prime Minister, was supposed to open the lecture series. He fell ill, however, and sent Lord Robert Cecil instead. Since it happened to get into the papers, I showed it to the detective and said, "If your Prime Minister trusts me, you can trust me too." But it had little or no effect on him — and rightly so. In the end I asked Seton-Watson to have a word with Scotland Yard, and after that the detective left me in peace.

But the head of Scotland Yard, Sir Basil Thompson, took an interest in me, and I visited him and explained to him what we were about. I was invited back in connection with the Countess Zanardi-Landi affair. The woman in question claimed to be the illegitimate daughter of the Empress Elisabeth and King Ludwig of Bavaria and had written a book about her life and origins. I read the book and found her descriptions of Vienna and the court rather vague. Sir Basil summoned me to hear my opinion on the matter. Her brother, clearly a Jew, was present at the interview and called his sister an imposter in so many words. I was thrown by the pictures of the woman and her daughters: she looked aristocratic and resembled the Austro-Bavarian royal family. I tried to meet her and wrote to her that I was interested in translating her book into Czech. When she failed to answer, I kept an eye out for her in the street: she lived only several houses away from us. The first time I saw her I realized immediately from her ears, the down on her cheeks, and her physiognomy how much she looked like her Jewish brother.

For the rest of the war my relations with the police were nothing if not friendly, but I kept having dreams about being chased by the Austrian police. I've had them even here, as President. Only recently have I been free of them.

*

Today I myself am amazed at how much I managed to get done. Every week I wrote or, rather, dictated an article for the *Sunday Times* combining facts and opinions. I wrote for other periodicals as well — *The Nation, The Spectator, New Europe* — and sent around short pieces through our press agency. I can't tell you how many memoranda I prepared, and the letters I wrote! Then there was my course at the University, lectures at various societies, at Cambridge, and at Oxford, where I stayed with the famous Cretologist Sir Arthur Evans and got to know Milyukov and Vinogradov. I went to Edinburgh to talk to the Belgian Consul, Professor Sarolea, and his editor Mrs. West (who published a fine paper called *Everyman,* which took an interest in our cause). I made regular visits to the Foreign Office to see Sir George Clerk, later the ambassador in Prague; Sir Maurice Bunsen, the former Austrian ambassador; and various Allied ambassadors, though I naturally spent more time with journalists and academics. There were Saturdays at Wickham Steed's, where newspapermen, officers, and diplomats came together; everyone who came to London would call on Wickham Steed and his wife, Rose, who wrote fine articles for the conservative *Morning Post.* I can't possibly remember the number of people I visited and tried to inform of our position, but even when we had trouble gaining public opinion I never thrust myself on people in high places. At first I was quite empty-handed and could promise nothing. All I had was my argument that the break-up of Austria-Hungary was in the interest of all Europe. I tried to see to it that the papers carried something against Austria and about us on a daily basis. We had to make our cause known; it was not enough to engage in politics in some ministry or other. And it was work, let me tell you, hard work: walks and visits, meetings and lectures, articles and letters, and couriers to be sent off and occasionally worried over when the English police made it hard on them. It happened sometimes when, after the button affair, we started getting couriers from America: as long as America was neutral, American citizens could go to both Vienna and Prague.

I had my principles when it came to propaganda, and I believe they were right. I felt we shouldn't malign the Germans, underestimate the enemy, distort reality, toot our own horn, make empty promises, or seek alms; we should let the facts speak for themselves and then point to them (thus and so is in your interest and hence your duty), sway people with ideas and arguments, keep a low personal profile, shun opportunism and anything that smacks of here-today-gone-tomorrow, maintain an overall plan and an overall standard — and one thing more, avoid harassing anyone.

Equally important was to accept money only from our own, even if others offered it. There were times when the till was nearly empty and Beneš would cable saying we needed such and such an amount, and that very day a check would come from our people in America. At first I was worried there were too few of us abroad, but it proved a good thing: our quarrels were fewer too.

Lies and exaggerations are the worst propaganda of all. Let me give you an example. When our friend Seton-Watson was a young man working on the history of Calvinists in Hungary, he had no idea — hardly anyone in Western Europe had — of the Hungarians' nationality policy. He liked the Hungarians. While gathering material in Pest, however, he came across documents dealing with the Slovaks and asked about them, thinking he might visit them. "There are no Slovaks," the Hungarians told him, "only a few shepherds in the highlands." But Seton-Watson got to know some, learned more from them, and went to Slovakia to see for himself. When he got back to Vienna, he said to Wickham Steed, wide-eyed with amazement, "Fancy that! The Hungarians lied to me! Lied to me!" And that was what induced him to study the national problems of the Slovaks and South Slavs and become the authority on Magyarization and Hungarian policy. No, lies do not pay in either public or private life.

*

I have had one or two close brushes with death. The first was in 1916, when Štefánik set up an appointment for me with Briand. I had just bought a ticket on the Channel steamer *Sussex* to go to Paris when I had a cable from Beneš saying the talk had been postponed. On that journey the *Sussex* was torpedoed by the Germans and went down.

The second was when on my way to Russia, I planned to sail from the Scottish port of Amble to Bergen in Norway. That time too I was unusually lucky. The ship I was waiting for never arrived; it had sunk. If I'd taken it, I'd have missed Štefánik, who was on his way back from Russia with important news for me. So I went back to London and saw not only Štefánik but also Beneš, who had come from Paris. A few days later I took a boat from Aberdeen in the company of two destroyers. During the night the boat suddenly heeled over and swung round quickly with a bang. Next morning the captain said we'd only just missed a floating mine: the boat had come round at the last minute.

I needed a new passport for Russia. Under a false name, of course. I picked a Danish name, Madwig. Danish because, as you'll remember, my wife's family, the Garrigues, came to America from Denmark; Madwig because there is a Danish philologist by that name. I made up the story of my life and committed it to memory to keep from contradicting myself if I fell into German hands. I was of Danish origin but had lived in the United States since childhood, and so on. But Sir Basil Thompson — I forget why — advised me to use another name. The name he pro-posed, Thomas George Marsden, is the name I use even now when traveling around the world. I wanted to keep my initials so as to avoid making a mistake when signing my name. Sir Basil also advised me to be particularly cautious in Sweden because it was full of German spies and the Swedish authorities might make a show of their neutrality by hand-ing me over to Austria or at least detaining me. So when I got to Stock-holm, I didn't even go to a hotel; I walked through the streets all day with Bohdan Pavlů, who had come from Petrograd to meet me.

I'd made ample preparation for the journey, obliterating all traces of my identity, removing all Paris and London labels from my clothes, going through every scrap of paper and apparel I was taking with me to make sure nothing could give me away. Then in Russia I found a collar on which a London laundry had written MASARYK in indelible ink! And I thought I was so prudent and practical!

I have often pondered such fateful moments in life. I have never looked upon Providence as something aristocratic, something that gives me more than others. Many people — all people, perhaps — enjoy a modicum of good fortune. The role of Providence in the development of states and nations is something else again, though states and nations are made up of individuals and individuals are the expression and medium of the whole. It's a difficult problem, a hard nut to crack, and I don't claim to explain it. Yes, it's a real philosophical conundrum.

1917

I went to Russia partly at the request of the Russian branch of our National Council — unifying our efforts in the Allied countries was an urgent task — and partly to recruit and organize our volunteers from Russian prisoner-of-war camps, that is, to turn them into an independent corps, which would *de facto* be a Czech army fighting against Austria. The greatest obstacle was the Russian bureaucracy, bureaucrats, as you know, being as much a part of armies as they are of offices. It was to be expected that with the fall of the tsar we would have an easier time of it and could count on the assistance of the new Minister of Foreign Affairs, Professor Milyukov, whom I knew well. So off I went to Russia. But as luck would have it, no sooner did I arrive than Milyukov resigned. Shortly thereafter civil war broke out. And in the midst of all that upheaval we had to organize our political and military campaign. It was a terrible trial.

Oddly enough, wherever I went in Russia there was shooting. In Petrograd I lived opposite the Telegraph and Telephone Bureau, which was under constant fire. Znamenskaya, the street where our National Council office was located, was close to my rooms near the Winter Palace, and I would walk there. The people at the Council were afraid I'd get hurt, so Šeba gave me their cook, Hůza, as a bodyguard. They brought him to me still in his apron and told me he would be going everywhere with me. I had a hard time getting used to him. I was in the habit of doing everything for myself — I even polished my own boots — and here was a fellow who insisted on doing everything for me. I just had to resign myself to it.

But Petrograd wasn't safe even with a bodyguard. Besides, what could he have done if a bullet had come our way? It was decided I should go to Moscow, where things were quiet, and the Council would follow me there. So off I went together with Kódl, whose name is known to readers of our legionnaire novels, but the moment I arrived in Moscow fighting broke out there as well. I left Hůza at the station to hire a cab for our luggage and went on foot to the Hotel National in the main square, where I had a room booked. When I got to the square, I ran into a cordon of soldiers. "Where are you going?" an officer called out to me. I said I was going to the Hotel National. "Impossible," he said. "There's shooting going on." I looked into the square and saw shooting on both sides: the side with the theater had been taken by the Bolsheviks, the other side was being held by Kerensky's men, and both sides were shooting with rifles and machine guns. The officer advised me to go to the Hotel Metropole. I set off. A man walking ahead of me suddenly broke into a run and slipped through a large door that had been opened a crack for him. It was the Hotel Metropole. I tried to slip in after him, but they slammed the door in my face. So I banged on it and shouted, "What are you doing? Open the door!" "Have you got a room here?" the porter shouted back. "We can't let you in otherwise. We're all booked up." I didn't want to lie, so I shouted, "Stop playing games and let me in!" He was so surprised he did let me in.

The Metropole was a cosmopolitan hotel de luxe for foreigners and rich Russians coming to Moscow on a spree. At the time it accommodated about five hundred people including staff. Approximately fifty of Kerensky's cadets were shooting down at the Bolsheviks from the attic, and the Bolsheviks in the theater were shooting back at them. When I got inside, the manager, or whoever he was, came up to me and said, "You can't stay here. We've no room and no food for you." "I'm not going anywhere," I said, "but I'm not asking you for anything. Just forget I'm here." So they let me sit there in my fur coat and took no further notice of me. Meanwhile the shooting continued and the guests all went down to the basement, where they had their midday and evening meal. I stayed where I was. In the evening the cook came and looked me over, wondering what kind of rare bird I was. We fell into conversation, and it turned out he had been expecting his father-in-law from the country and had a room ready for him. Since his father-in-law couldn't get to the hotel, he offered me the room. Then he gave me a meal as well.

The room was on the second or third floor and around the corner from the action, so a bullet could come in only by ricocheting off the buildings opposite. Still, I dragged the mattress down from the bed and slept on the floor in a corner. During the day I wandered around the hotel, wondering what Hůza and the Moscow Czechs expecting me were up to. No one could leave the hotel, and as the telephone was in the entrance hall and thus in the line of fire we were cut off from the outside world. It was odd. I've never experienced such long days. It wasn't so bad when the Bolsheviks used only rifles and machine guns, but after a few days they started firing cannons. Before long the whole frontage of the hotel, all the upper stories, was badly damaged. Most of the guests moved down to the basement, but I couldn't stand it there: the noise and the stench, the women and children crying. A Pole who'd been through the bombardment of Przemyśl said that it wasn't nearly so frightening as this. Still, I crawled (I literally had to crawl because of the debris and the shooting) my way up to my room every night.

One scene I shall never forget. I can see it as if it were yesterday. I was standing in the corner of my room by the window, peering outside to see what was going on, when I saw a youth dash into the street and try to cross it. But suddenly he fell, fell flat on his face, his arms spread wide. I remember thinking, "If I were a doctor, I'd be able to tell where he'd been hit from the way he fell." There he lay on the pavement, his face to the ground, his fur cap a step away. A small stream of blood flowed from under his face, then a second and a third — seven in all. I counted them. As I stood there watching, a raven swooped down, perched on the cap, and stared at the boy. I was terribly afraid it would start pecking at him, but there was nothing I could do; I had no way of shooing it away. There was a Red Cross ambulance around the corner, but they didn't come for the boy because of all the shooting. They did take pity on him in the end, though, waving their Red Cross flag and carrying him off. I don't know if he was still alive. And there were any number of scenes like that. . .

Since, as I've said, the hotel telephone was in the entrance hall, where bullets were flying, we were forbidden to use it, but I finally sneaked up to it anyway and got through to our people, who all thought I was dead. Hůza once tried to bring me a change of clothes, but had to turn back. Then one night after the cannonade Kerensky's cadets withdrew from the hotel, and when the Bolsheviks started firing again the hotel surrendered. The following day — a Saturday, I believe — the Bolsheviks agreed to let the guests leave. The Russians among them chose a Pole as their negotiator; the foreign guests (of whom there were more than forty) chose me. We gathered up the weapons left in the hotel and piled them together, though the Pole hid some of the loaded revolvers and ammunition in anticipation of a shoot-out (in which case it would scarcely have mattered whether we defended ourselves or not). He was chiefly afraid of an attack on the women, which would have led to wholesale slaughter. Only a few of us knew about the hiding place.

The Bolsheviks occupied the hotel and took away the weapons. A motley group they were, with rifles on strings and the like. They put us under guard. One of the soldiers reached out for a ring I had on my tie. It was made of aluminum, I believe, and had a red stone set in it. Our boys had made it out of a percussion cap and given it to me as a souvenir, but because I wear no ring but my wedding ring I fastened it to my tie. I showed the soldier it was only metal and glass and told him it was a keepsake but he could have it if he so desired. He did not. I asked him in jest if he would let me go soon. "I'll let you go if I like," he replied, "and I'll cut your throat if I like." He did not cut my throat. Several of the guests bribed the guards, but I'm not good at it; it's so humiliating.

The worst part of it was when the guards got drunk on wine they found in the cellar. I went to their commander and asked him to replace them. He did as I asked. After a long night a commission — led by a student, to judge by his clothes — came to inspect our passports. One of the guests was a Latvian socialist who knew my work on Marxism, and he saw to it I was not harassed.

Anyway, after a week in the hotel I was released. I went to stay with my fellow countrymen Országh and Rixy and went back to work organizing the corps. When our boys went to see the hotel where I had stayed, one of them took a key and eventually put it in the Turčansky Svatý Martin Museum.

From Moscow I moved on to Kiev because our corps were encamped there. I put up at the Hotel Paris on the Kreshchatik, but no sooner did I arrive than the Bolsheviks surrounded the city, and when the time allotted for surrender was up they opened fire on the city. Dr. Girsa took me to the Saint George Hospital, saying I'd be safer there, but our meetings were at the Hotel Paris, so it didn't really matter: I had to go there every day anyway. Once a grenade landed in the room next door to ours; it hit the wall, fell to the floor, and lay there without going off. It was a good two feet long. No harm was done, except a piece of plaster hit the head of a member of the family dining there.

Then the Bolsheviks advanced into the city and fought in the streets. The route to our office followed the main boulevard and a cross street by the name of Proreznaya, if I'm not mistaken. One day I was walking along the cross street with Hůza during the shooting. We took cover against the buildings on the side the bullets were coming from. True, we could have been hit by chimney pots and roof tiles, but we had no choice. A grenade happened to fall and explode in a nearby courtyard, so we went to have a look at it.

When we reached the main boulevard, an officer ran up to us, waving and shouting, "*Opasno!* You're in danger! Get back!" All along the boulevard there was a rat-a-tat-tat of bullets hailing down on the pavement. "We're as likely to get hit if we go back," I said to Hůza, "so let's go forward." And we dashed across the boulevard.

One day Klecanda and I were standing in front of the railway station waiting to meet the Bolshevik commander when bang! a bullet hit a telephone pole an inch above our heads. Two boys had been playing with a loaded gun in a nearby courtyard; the gun went off and killed one of them, and the bullet then sailed all the way to us.

The only time I was truly afraid was when the soldiers in Moscow got drunk. That could have been a disaster. Otherwise I wasn't afraid, or if I was I didn't show it. I couldn't, because of our soldiers. What kind of commander would I have been if they could tell I was scared?

I could go on about all this and various individual experiences, but I've forgotten many of the details and, to be frank, I have no desire to recall them. I've got plenty of other things on my mind. . .

With the Troops in Russia

In Russia, believe it or not, I was even busier than in England. There was no time to write, only to act, though there was a lot of talking too, because in Russia you can't get anywhere without gibber-jabber. Russian meetings run from morning to night; I never got out into the fresh air until the wee hours. I was constantly on the go, visiting the Russian Staff Headquarters, our regiments, etc. It was exhausting, let me tell you. Once the train I was in had an accident, a broken axle or something, but luckily it was slowing down to come into a station and so nothing happened, except that we had to stand crammed together in other cars for the rest of the journey.

We had no end of problems in Russia, the worst of which were with the authorities, which were incapable of understanding our cause: they kept thinking of us as Austrians and traitors to our emperor, and if we had betrayed the emperor we might betray the tsar. We wanted them to let us turn our prisoners of war into a volunteer army against the Germans. They finally allowed us to form several regiments, but we wanted to make them an entire corps. I know why they didn't like the idea: they were afraid that if they gave in to us they'd have to give in to the Poles, and they didn't trust the Poles. Besides, they had few enough uniforms or arms for their own men and would have to equip ours. And many Russians didn't want our men to fight; they preferred using them as skilled workers in factories and mines, on the railways, in the fields. So Klecanda and I and a few others were constantly going to Head-quarters and making the rounds of the ministries — it was a bitter pill to swallow. Milyukov, who, as you'll remember, resigned the very day I arrived in Petrograd, would have been well disposed towards us, but I had to negotiate with the generals, men like Brusilov, Alexeev and, most of all, Dukhonin, the Russian chief of staff, a fine soldier and the man we finally came to terms with.

Perhaps our greatest support came from public opinion, when our men fought so well at Zborov. I happened to be negotiating then at Russian Staff Headquarters in Mogilev and had a number of talks, notably with Brusilov, who bowed at the waist and said, "I bow in deep respect for your soldiers." I was glad we could do something for him after the war when as an exile he took the cure at Karlovy Vary. After he died, his wife sent me his personal icon wrapped in a cloth rent by bullets. He had carried it with him everywhere for protection, and he bequeathed it to me.

When at last we had our corps, Dukhonin asked me whom we wished to command it, and I chose General Shokorov, a reliable military official. Soon thereafter the Bolsheviks killed Dukhonin and disfigured his corpse. At the funeral his widow told me Dukhonin had wanted to command our army himself. It had never entered my mind that the Chief of General Staff might be interested in commanding our corps! We must at least show our gratitude to his widow for the good will and respect he showed our soldiers.

Trouble with the Bolsheviks began the moment the corps was formed. We had agreed upon armed neutrality, and I had got them to grant us passage through Siberia so the troops could sail for France. By the time I left for Siberia, they were talking either of disarming us or winning us over to their side, which meant endless negotiations with the commissars, the military, and all manner of people.

We naturally had trouble with our own people as well. First of all there were the old, half-Russianized emigrants. Every emigration takes on the psychology of the country where it lives: the character of the Czech colony in Paris differed from the character of the Czech colony in America, which differed from the character of the Czech colony in Russia. It was simply a fact of life. A few powerful Czechs in Russia had accepted the tsarist system hook, line, and sinker. Some of them informed against me at the various ministries and had quite a bit of influence over their fellow Czechs as well. All that had to be sorted out.

Then we had trouble with our soldiers as well. There were volunteers from the Czech colony in Russia and volunteers from prisoner-of-war camps. There were conflicts to be settled between the original volunteer unit known as the Družina, the volunteers from Serbia and the Dobrogea region, and the new regiments made up of POWs. Others argued over whether we should go to the Caucasus, to the Romanian front, or via Arkhangelsk to France, yet others over whether the command should be Russian or Czech and whether the officers should mess together with the men. It was things like these I had to deal with. What did I tell them? I told them it didn't matter a whit who was in command as long as commands were obeyed, or whether officers and men messed together — they could eat wherever they pleased — as long as the food was decent. There were demagogic officers who harangued the men at table and men who had no desire to go into battle; there were problems with provisions. And all around us Russian soldiers were deserting, the Russian army was disintegrating. Such were the conditions we worked under when putting together our corps.

Not only that. Prisoners of war are naturally somewhat demoralized. They are unnerved by the humiliation and injustice of it all, by being uprooted. Besides, once a soldier has thrown away his gun he wants to have done with war. Our recruiting efforts in prisoner-of-war camps did not always go smoothly. Certain camp commanders — non-Russians, for the most part — did their best to make things hard for us. The literature circulated among POWs for enlistment purposes was full of ideals likely to scare them away: "You will suffer hunger, you will lie lice-infected in the trenches." That was what was in store for them if they joined forces with us and all they wanted was a full stomach and better living conditions than they'd had as POWs.

Then there were those who argued with their officers because they felt volunteers didn't need to obey blindly. They were encouraged by demagogues who set up military councils and committees on the Bolshevik model and tried to run the army by consensus. Natural as it all was, it was sometimes quite painful. We had a colonel, a Russian, who spouted Hus and brotherhood because he thought it would get him promoted. Well, I "bit him through," as the Russians say, that is, I blocked his promotion. His men nearly revolted. There was a great deal of that kind of thing. The men who had undergone Bolshevization carried on an agitprop campaign against our army and the loan meant to finance it, but no sooner did the Germans advance on Kiev than they all ran to join up: the army had become our protection.

I can tell you this: your Czech is a good soldier under fire. He is uncommonly brave and resourceful and can get himself out of a fix. But when he's not in one, he manages to find one. He's not always good at holding his ground, and he falls apart when he has nothing to do, which was the case both before and at the end of the Siberian campaign. Yet even a better equipped and organized army would have fought no better than we did. All I cared about was that they should fight well until we reached France. The business of brotherhood and the rights of a volunteer army was fine with me so long as the men were ready for combat. We organized courses for the officers, drills for the men, and all manner of activities — making clothes, making shoes, smoking meat, operating a printing press, playing sports, putting on plays, running a post office, a bank — to keep them occupied and prevent them from deserting. Maintaining the food supply was extremely difficult: the Ukrainian peasants refused to accept rubles; they said the Germans had paid in nails. Since paper money was of no use to them, we developed a primitive form of barter. Things were better in Siberia. And, of course, as soon as our boys were under fire they made top-notch soldiers: they were fighting for their lives.

They were fond of me and accepted me as their commander-in-chief, mainly, I think, because I bawled them out from time to time — in the military you have to say what's on your mind — and perhaps because I was brave. Crowds of them went to see the badly damaged Hotel Metropole where I had stayed; they made up legends about me, said I was fearless. In fact, I was frightened many times; I just never let it show. It was for their sake I walked through streets under fire. They completely forgot I was a professor. I enjoyed spending time with them. Soldiers have a lot in common with children; like children they need to be treated fairly, openly, straight from the shoulder. Because they must follow orders even unto death, they must have a genuine, unhypocritical respect for the man who gives them. Military parades are more for the rank and file than for the commander. I don't like war, but I do like soldiers.

My greatest concern was where to use our corps to the best effect. The Russian front no longer existed, but there were five hundred thousand well-armed German troops in the West because the Germans didn't trust the Bolsheviks. At first the Bolsheviks were supposedly on our side against the Germans, but the Allies didn't want that, and rightly so. Then Lenin went against Trotsky's will and made peace with the Germans. Now how in the world could we fight our way home through the German front — an army of fifty thousand men, no artillery or matériel to speak of, a completely inadequate food supply, and a revolution in full swing in the rear? Or wage a war of attrition against the Bolsheviks? The tsar had fallen, his entire administration was in ruins, his vast empire was in the throes of a revolution — how could we with fifty thousand soldiers suppress so large a movement provoked by the inadequacies of the old regime?

When in the autumn of 1917 France wanted to fling our soldiers onto the Romanian front, I went to Mirceşti near Jassy and found scarcely any fighting going on. They merely fired a shot or two in my honor, so to speak, and the Germans responded in an equally unwarlike manner. I learned from my talks with the Romanian and French officers that there wasn't enough meat or bread for full rations, in other words, their food supply was giving out. Besides, I sensed Romania was thinking of peace, and I was right. What could we do there? I decided to go elsewhere, even if it meant disagreeing with Clemenceau.

The only reasonable course to take was to move our troops to the French front, where every man was needed. I could see we'd never get there from Arkhangelsk: transportation was poor and whatever ships we could muster the Germans would torpedo in no time. The shortest route to France and home was the longest: across Siberia and around the world. So that's what I ordered, going on ahead myself through Siberia as quartermaster to show it could be done.

But first I negotiated an armed neutrality with Commissar Frich, the Bolsheviks' first generalissimo and a former university professor. Our troops were to be armed. I had it in black and white. I issued orders to the effect that our troops were not to intervene in internal Russian affairs (or we'd never get out of Russia) but that if any Slav party were to attack them they had permission to defend themselves. By this time we were in a state of war with the Germans and the Hungarians, because I had got the French to declare our army officially part of theirs. The only ones who could stand in our way were the Bolsheviks, which is why I said "Slav party." The reason for the neutrality was obvious: the Bolsheviks were providing us with food or at least not holding us back from foraging.

I left Moscow on 7 March, which happened to be my birthday. By the good graces of Lady Paget I was given a seat in the English Red Cross train taking the English Red Cross mission out of Russia. I had only a hard seat, but luckily Hůza managed to find me a mattress in Moscow. The journey lasted a month. On the way I thought out and wrote my *New Europe,* studied my English traveling companions, and debated with the Bolshevik conductor. Once, the train had to stop because there was fighting in the countryside ahead of us. From time to time our fuel ran out and wood had to be cut for the locomotive. There was no one better than Hůza for that.

I was in a hurry to get to America because I felt a peace conference was in the offing, but I had to stop in Japan first to get in touch with the European Allies and let the Japanese authorities know that at least a part of our troops would be shipping out from Japan. I was unable to study Japan; I had no time to look around.

We had a hard time of it in Russia, but we did a good job of it and did not go home empty-handed. We had something genuinely our own to show for our pains: the first real — if still extra-territorial — part of our future country.

The War's End

I sailed from Japan to Vancouver on the *Empress of Asia.* Both my fellow countrymen and American newspapermen were waiting for me everywhere I went in America. It took me a while to get used to my American fame.

The country had lived in a state of feverish excitement throughout the war. It was all so new to Americans. They felt a new bond with Europe and the world as a whole. Besides, they were cheering on our legions, which had begun to fight their way across Russia and Siberia by then. I knew our men and was certain they would come through with flying colors, but Americans have an unusual admiration for heroism of every kind, so the march of our fifty thousand across a whole continent made a great impression on them.

It was my fourth visit to America. The first was when I went to bring Miss Garrigue home in 1878, the second and third when I went to lecture — in 1902 and 1907. I had thus seen America grow from her pioneer days. Yes, I like America. Not so much the countryside: ours is more beautiful. The American countryside is — how shall I put it? — it's like American fruit: their fruit for some reason always tastes unripe to me; ours is mellower, sweeter. I think it has to do with the thousand years of cultivation behind everything here: America's countryside isn't as ripe as ours somehow. For the American farmer, so well-equipped, the soil is a factory rather than an object of love, as it still is for us.

One thing that appeals to me about America is how open the people are. Like America our country has its good and bad people, of course, but Americans are more open about being bad. Your American bandit is ruthless, merciless: he doesn't hide behind a screen of morality or patriotism; he's an out-and-out crook. The good ones are just as energetic about doing what they think is right, be it for humanitarian, religious, or cultural causes; they are more enterprising in their goodness than we are. There's still a pioneer spirit there in keeping with their wild landscape.

I'm not surprised that America is highly industrialized and highly efficient. After all, she has a hundred million people to supply with goods; she has to produce on a large scale — it comes with the wide open spaces. But I don't see much difference between their capitalism and ours: their billionaire is our millionaire — only the proportions vary. People talk about the race for the dollar, as if we were any better. The only difference is that here in Europe we race for pennies more than dollars and we're reticent about it, ashamed of it, which is no more virtuous, only less impetuous.

Americans are machine-crazy, people say. But machines have their good side as well as bad, as do efficiency experts and the like. There's nothing wrong with machines that relieve people of hard, debilitating labor. More should be made of that than of financial gain.

Still, I found the tempo of American life a bit strange. I need enough space around everything I do to let me think it through properly.

Our workers may not have the American get-up-and-go, but they do a good, accurate job of things. We place quality above quantity.

Americans have more respect for physical labor than we do: your American student will spend his summers working in the fields or waiting on tables. We tend to overrate education, especially its scholarly aspect. The American worker has more freedom than ours, more elbow-room, and if he's good at what he does he'll have his own Ford car and bungalow. That's why America has no socialism in our sense of the word.

I see no harm in our becoming Americanized; we've been Europeanizing America for centuries. They have the right. Besides, even as we Americanize ourselves, America is Europeanizing itself: according to what I've read, two million Americans come to Europe every year, and if Europe has anything of value for their lives they'll take it home with them. Read the latest American writers and you'll see how roundly they condemn the errors of the American way of life, its superficialities. I wish our writers were as frank about ours! The only future is one in which Europe will be a match for America and America for Europe. In short, America gave me much food for thought. I learned many, many valuable things there.

*

All the time I was in America I made conscious preparations for the peace conference. The first thing we had to do was strengthen Czech-Slovak unity. The second thing was to get the Ruthenians to join us voluntarily. It was a brand-new project, one that originated in America, where I saw what having a territorial bridge to a future democratic Russia or Ukraine would mean for us. I made no attempt to talk the Ruthenian representatives into anything; I simply put it this way: You can join us or the Hungarians or the Poles — the choice is yours. They chose us. The next thing we had to do was similar to what we'd had to do in Europe: unite the smaller European nations in their fight for freedom, that is, talk to the Poles, Ruthenians, Serbs, Croats, Romanians, and others. The result was the joint Declaration of Independence in Philadelphia. But we also needed to win over the American people, so there were all kinds of meetings, consultations, lectures, and more or less formal rallies and conferences. There was no getting around it, though; we had to do something about public opinion, the general public knowing little about us and all but nothing about the Slovaks. The war with the Germans had been popular in America, but the tangled national problems of Central Europe were quite alien to people. Fortunately, the Czechs in America had been carrying on an anti-Austrian propaganda campaign since the war began, and when the Czech Legions in Siberia captured the attention of the whole world we were ready to take advantage of it. The main thing was to waste no time because the war was drawing to a close. In fact, it ended half a year sooner than I had expected.

Once public opinion had been taken care of, I began negotiating with official circles: Lansing, Colonel House, and the like. My old friend Charles Crane was of great help to me: his son was Lansing's secretary. President Wilson I met met four times, I think. My first impression of him was one of such perfect neatness that I said to myself he must have a wife who loves him. We understood each other very well: we were both professors, after all. He was firm about his principles, but open to objections. He knew who I was: we had been in indirect contact before I came to America. I saw he would not be at home in European affairs, that his direct approach would keep him from being understood by European statesmen. I warned him not to come to Europe for the Peace Conference, but he would have none of it: he was too bent on his plan for the League of Nations to think of the drawbacks.

In May 1918 my daughter Olga came over from England. Boats were forbidden to carry women and children at the time because of submarine warfare, and the only way she could obtain passage was by presenting a note from President Wilson to the effect that she was a courier carrying dispatches for him. She was the only woman in a convoy of eight ships. I lived in Washington most of the time and would go horseback riding in Rock Creek Park for a bit of air and exercise. In fact, I nearly broke my neck trying to jump the highest obstacle. After that, I wasn't allowed to go riding alone. I was also given my first car. It was a small Dodge. I remember driving it — or attempting to drive it — through the streets on Armistice Day. I had never seen such mass rejoicing, people cheering and singing, hugging one another, tooting their horns; all New York was snowed under with confetti. We Czechs lack the Americans' ability to be so wildly, childishly exuberant.

When I received the telegram telling me I'd been elected president — well, the possibility simply hadn't occurred to me before. If I ever thought of what I'd do when I went home, I pictured myself as a journalist, and all I could think of when I got the news was the problem of leaving: who would come with me and so on. I left on 20 November, which happened to be my wife's birthday. The voyage back was my first holiday in four years. I could play chess with my daughter (I haven't held a chessman in my hand since then) and stroll up and down the deck, watching the sea and thinking how it had all come about, and how happy I was. Dear God, we'd actually done it!

THE REPUBLIC

The Old Oak

One thing that surprised me coming home from the war was how my friends, my contemporaries, had aged. I'd been so engrossed in the war — from the smallest minutiae to the end result — that I quite forgot everything else, and it wasn't until I saw the change in others that I realized I must have aged too!

Look at that oak. People say it's nine hundred years old, and see how strong it is, how full of life! Neither its size nor its age keeps it from putting out new leaves or blossoms. Well, that's how people should age. It shouldn't be a feat to live to a hundred, but no tricks or gimmicks will get us there, that's for sure. Fresh air and sunshine; moderate food and drink; a moral life and a job involving muscles, heart, and brain; people to care for and a goal to strive for — that's the macrobiotic recipe of success. Oh, and a keen interest in life, because an interest in life is tantamount to life itself, and without it and without love, life ceases to exist.

We tend to measure life by too one-sided a standard: its length rather than its greatness; we think more of extending life than filling it. Many people are afraid of death, yet have no idea that they and many others like them are *de facto* living only half a life, a life that is empty, loveless, joyless. In the awareness of truth, in a moral order, in active love we can find a modicum of eternity here below. There is nothing wrong with increasing the length of a life, but we must also increase its value. I have a recurrent dream — I don't know where it comes from, perhaps a painting — of a ship at sea and an angel with a clock bending over it. Every so often a drop trickles down the clock into the sea, and the angel says, "Another minute gone." I've always taken it as a warning: Get on with your work, do what you have to do while you have the time.

Many people age because it takes no doing and they have no wish to do anything more. Keeping young does not mean merely holding on; it means growing, opening up. Each year should be like climbing a rung on a ladder. I keep close watch to see if I'm aging: I test my intellectual powers, my memory, my coordination, and so on. The moment I see any of them starting to fail, I'll make room for the younger generation.

*

A few words about caring for the body. If I had my way, I'd pretty much do without doctors, but if people can't look after themselves, they need sawbones to do it for them. Still, every educated person should keep tabs on his body and watch his diet. That's not materialism; materialism is eating and drinking whatever and whenever you feel like it. The first rule is moderation: eat and drink a lot less than most people do. If you want to know about me, well, I eat three times a day. For breakfast I have fruit, then lightly buttered toast with jam, an occasional strip of bacon, and about half a glass of unsweetened tea. I used to have soft-boiled eggs, but apparently they're not good for you. At midday I have a few spoonfuls of thick soup, a small slice of meat with plenty of vegetables, a piece of pastry, some fruit, and black coffee. For supper I now get by with only a bowl of milk pudding or a bun and a cup of milk colored with a dash of coffee. That's all I need. I don't give guests more than that either or, rather, I make only one concession: a simple fish course or something similar. They say it helps to stimulate the appetite, though why that should be necessary I'm sure I don't know: isn't appeasing natural hunger more important? I eat nothing at all between meals, though at five I will take a sip of tea if I have guests. The stomach needs rest like any other part of the body, and the only time it can get it is when we fast. Most people work their stomachs to death; overeating is like lugging around a heavy burden. Doctors have started warning people against putting on weight: overweight people are less likely to live long because they overstrain their organs. Besides, excessive overweight is unattractive, and attractive people are part of a humanitarian program.

As far as drinking goes, I have never touched hard liquor. Wine I drank from childhood — I was born in wine country — beer I didn't learn to drink until I moved to town. Later, just before I turned fifty, I realized that alcohol is totally useless — harmful, in fact — and stopped drinking altogether. After my last illness the doctors coerced me into drinking a glass of wine before meals. Not only did I find it distasteful, I noticed after a bit of experimenting that I didn't need it and even did better without it. As president I've tried to get my guests to give up wine and beer with their meals, but to no avail. Oh well, to each his own. I don't make a religion of abstinence, but from time to time I try to make my fellow citizens see that immoderate indulgence in alcohol is, to be blunt, stupid.

The rest of my daily regime is quite simple. Immediately after rising I have a cold bath and do my own variation of the Sokol exercises. I make sure I either walk or go riding for an hour or two every day. I can still manage two to three hours in the saddle, and until a few years ago I would ride five hours at a go. Cleanliness is important too — clean teeth, a clean mouth, a clean body, and clean air. As for smoking, I once smoked as a boy to appear manly. It was 1866, and I wanted to show the Prussians I was a Czech, so I rolled cigarettes out of red, white, and blue paper and puffed away whenever they were around. I took up cigarettes again while at the University (though what I enjoyed most was rolling them well). Smoking and drinking are not needs, they are habits. If we want to bring up healthy children, we can't just explain what is healthful and what isn't, we can't just preach; we have to inculcate practical, healthful habits in them.

I once read somewhere that death is nothing but a bad habit. I don't want to go into death just now, but premature aging and a number of illnesses are certainly nothing but bad habits. I believe that just as people can expect to have more and more control over natural forces they can expect to have more and more control over their health and habits and that we shall one day look upon many of our present maladies with the horror we now reserve for medieval or Asiatic plagues.

Modern medicine is right to stop concentrating on cures and start dealing with prevention and education.

Being President

I was completely unprepared to become president. Even though I'd been recognized as head of our government abroad, even though I was certain we'd emerge from the war a free nation and I'd return home, I hadn't had time to ponder what to do with myself. Go back to teaching? Combine teaching with journalism and a seat in Parliament?

When they elected me president in November 1918, I said to myself, "Well, that's settled" and didn't worry my head about it: I had too many other things to take care of before leaving America. Not until I was on the boat did I start going over the new situation in my head: comparing the American and Swiss Republics, putting together a list of people with political and administrative experience, and thinking out details of a structural nature — the form the state apparatus should take and such. I had been analyzing the state — its form and function — for years, and as a member of Parliament I had studied the makeup of Austria-Hungary and its political and cultural strengths in great detail. I was at a considerable disadvantage, however, in that I was unfamiliar with what had been going on at home. Moreover, I had to keep up with events in London, Paris, and Rome, knowing I'd be visiting them and the political personalities in charge of building the new Europe at the Peace Conference. It was a lot to keep in my mind. And then I had to learn the formalities of being head of state.

When I first arrived home I didn't feel very well; in fact, I didn't think I had long to live. It must have been the exertion and excitement of the war and the bouts of influenza I'd gone through: I had to see to it that there should be a certain continuity to everything, that nothing should upset the work we were doing abroad. But now the time had come to reap the harvest of that work, of the many measures we had taken and contacts we had made. Such was my main concern. Yet I had to adjust to the new conditions: the government had been formed, as had the revolutionary National Assembly; new laws and institutions were beginning to appear. Fortunately I'd known nearly all the people involved in politics for years and knew what to expect of each of them. But there was so much more to learn, something new every day. It's not easy being the first president of a new country, a country with no tradition of self-rule and representation. I saw mistakes being made; I made some myself. Take this, for example. Forgetting I was president, I promised my friends that on the day after I took the oath of office I would meet them at the café where we had held our political discussions in 1914. But no sooner did I set off for town from the Castle than I was surrounded by flocks of people. I had to learn to be president, and I'm learning still. I constantly come up against situations forcing me to make new decisions.

Yes, it took a great deal of thought to determine what the president of a democratic state is or is supposed to be. When the constitution was being drawn up, many people imagined the function of the president to be more or less symbolic: they thought he would *de facto* have no say in political affairs. That would have been analogous to the strictly constitutional (English) monarchy. But our first constitution was no finished product, not in theory or in practice; it took over the old state machinery (which was the right thing to do!). What was new in it came from the pressure of radically altered circumstances. I made my presence felt through Švehla and a few others; for example, I stipulated that the president should have the constitutional right not only to ratify governmental and parliamentary proposals but also to take part in governmental deliberations and, if need be, even speak out in Parliament. I was also concerned about the technical expertise of the administration and government, which is why we have a combined parliamentary and professional government with a stable cohort of state officials (like Švehla and Beneš) at the top.

I believe we have a good constitution, but the most important thing was and is to bring the letter of the law to life. There are certain points in our constitution, as in every other, that are unclear, certain things that might be different. We have far too many members of Parliament, for example: England shows we could have done with two hundred. But amending the constitution is a ticklish business. Take America, where in the hundred and forty years since the constitution was framed only nineteen amendments have been passed of the more than two thousand proposed. Moreover, the amendments are actually supplements — the women's franchise, for instance; the original text remains in force. As I say, what matters is not merely the letter of the law but how we interpret it and put it into practice. All laws, the Constitution included, lag behind the inexorable progression of events, but the need for new codification eventually makes itself felt. What is known as customary law is not limited to the dawn of civilization; it is still very much alive, though in altered guises.

No matter what I do, I take into account how it will shape *praeiudicium,* or custom. It hasn't always been easy. Tradition must be created consciously. The inevitable formalities of government, for example. I have tried to imbue even them with a democratic spirit commensurate with the times and the genius of our nation. I wish our people were more aware of the necessity for symbols: political life, much like religious life, finds intellectual and ideological expression in symbols. Until taking on the presidency, I lived as private a life as possible; now I've had to make my peace with those guards downstairs and parades and receptions and all the other ceremonies. "What can you do?" I sometimes say to myself. "It's par for the course." But we've done well in this respect: the way our Republic handles formalities and protocol is in many ways exemplary. I myself live as I would wish every citizen to live. My only extravagance is books, but they serve the public.

As I say, I find being constantly under surveillance and in the public eye my greatest sacrifice, my greatest burden, but I've also been plagued by numerous daily political and administrative problems. Think of the early days of the Republic and the financial chaos, the civil unrest and coups d'état in almost every neighboring state. We've nearly forgotten what was more dangerous — the economic breakdown, the wave of communism, or the desperate attempts by the deposed classes to regain power. We must still be on our guard against errors old and new. And while today we take it for granted that our country managed to survive it all more or less peacefully and even build up our constitution and institutions, at the time we had to keep our wits about us and use our heads. I had a weekly conference — even several weekly conferences —

with Švehla, Tusar, Rašín, and other high-ranking officials. Beneš was abroad, so the correspondence was voluminous. The consultations we had, the meals we took together (which were just so many more consultations), the walks, the talks!

Still, I enjoy looking back on those times; they helped to give me a clear, concrete picture of the importance of personality in politics and the state. A solid platform is all well and good, but it must also have an honest, brave, and wise individual behind it, one who has the courage of responsibility. That is why I always pay more attention to people than to slogans. We are much too given to slogans; it's probably another of our legacies from Austria-Hungary: under Austria, when Vienna did the governing and administering instead of us, we acquired the unhealthy habit of using slogans. I know you can't do without them in politics, but now that our state is our own, our slogans — or, if you like, our ideals — must be embodied in concrete, well-thought-out requests and suggestions, and in practical programs. You can tell from our newspapers (*all* our newspapers) the kind of *à peu près* thinking we're capable of: fuzzy, negative, polemical, unconstructive. Not that I have anything against criticism. Heavens! I've spent most of my life criticizing one thing or another! But what I want is constructive criticism, sober and practical. Not even a revolution can be purely negative; it must have a positive grounding and preparation. How, I ask you, can totally negative criticism foster reform?

Naturally I still have conferences with our leading politicians and ministers. All the time, in fact. I try to keep my eye on everything, though I meddle as little as possible with the administrative side of things: the ministers need to learn by experience just as I did. Often, even daily, I say to myself, "Thirty more years of peaceful, rational, efficient progress and the country will be secure." But I can count on my fingers the men with the strength and experience to lead us through those thirty years. (True, I don't know the younger people.) I'm not only talking about politicians, I'm talking about statesmen, and we are so low on the latter that — let me tell you straight out — we all need to work overtime. So let's be careful not to lose or even willfully abuse anyone who has proved his worth.

We still have a great deal to learn. First and foremost, we must learn the art of judging our members of Parliament, politicians, journalists, and officials by the high standards of statesmanship, and you're no statesman if you can't look down the road a bit and make ready for what lies beyond. But perhaps nothing is so important in either politics or life as understanding people, recognizing who is genuine and has a calling, but also who is false and merely trying to elbow his way to the fore. Every major change in regime brings its share of upstarts, loud-mouths, and false prophets to the surface. We have ours. By their fruits ye shall know them, and in the end they will all be revealed. In spite of everything dividing us into camps and parties, we all want a sensible, honorable political system, and even in politics twice two is and always shall be four.

I have always considered foreign policy as important as domestic policy. I certainly thought so just after the war. In foreign policy we must be doubly careful to look ahead, prepare for things to come, and avoid being caught off-guard. Questions of the future can never be narrowly defined; the only way we can hazard a guess about the future is by casting our nets wide and taking all the relevant forces and factors into account. You must know if you want to predict, as Comte puts it. Foreign policy is and should remain a matter of a powerful and self-consistent concept of the state and the world, and yet few people realize how much spadework and invisible initiatives genuine foreign policy requires. For me, at any rate, it represents a never-ending effort.

During the war I realized the practical value of personal contacts and straightforward personal communication in politics as a whole and international politics in particular. Human feeling and trust are better arguments than any amount of cunning. In the realm of foreign relations the president sometimes functions in a formal, official capacity, but far more often his role is a private one. I am of course aware that the concept of "privacy" has no legal definition. But because we have had so little contact with the outside world, we more than most peoples need to cultivate friendly relations with the untold number of visitors who come to us out of an interest in our country and institutions. Few people have any idea how much time I devote to this.

A good number of the people who visit me have come to see the author of books on politics and others issues they find interesting rather than the president; in other words, I serve as writer, schoolmaster, and journalist. I don't like lecturing or preaching — I much prefer hearing what they have to say — but like it or not, I have to earn their confidence. Good, friendly relations with the outside world make for healthy economic relations.

Another important aspect of my politics is refurbishing the Castle, by which I mean turning it into a historical monument, the emblem of our once old, now new state and a symbol of both its past and future. *In concreto,* I wish to transform the monarchist Castle into a democratic Castle.

From the outset I've devoted a great deal of attention to our army. I started studying military affairs while still a member of the Austrian Parliament, but went into them much more deeply during the war, when I had to gauge the results of the hostilities and organize our corps in Russia. I am a convinced pacifist, but I love the army. Even if there were no more war, there would still be a need for two basic military virtues in every man worthy of the name: discipline and courage. I may want peace, but that doesn't mean I will meet aggression unarmed. On the contrary. What I want is a practical peace, not a utopian one, and that means I'll dedicate the combined power of my brain and my love of country and humanity to keep the peace, but also, if attacked, to fight a war. We must be brave and manly and as strong as possible. There has never been the slightest contradiction between my humanist ideals and my efforts in defense of the state. We need peace to build our country and to provide everyone with the greatest personal happiness. That is why we must work for a durable, judicious peace. Besides, all other countries and nations need peace as much as we do. The new Europe is like a laboratory built over the great graveyard of the World War, and a laboratory calls for the cooperation of all. Democracy — modern democracy — is in its infancy. Shutting our eyes to the adherents and exponents of the old aristocracy and monarchy still at work would be a grave error.

We may always have armies in one form or another and will certainly have them for a long time to come. What I mean is that a nation needs a trained body of brave, hardy men ready to be posted anywhere at a moment's notice and work on the scene of natural disasters and the like or fight in defense of their country.

The issue of capital punishment has always weighed heavy on me. I have lost many nights pondering over whether to sign a death warrant, and the days when I have done so I mark with a black cross on my calendar. I have looked carefully into whether capital punishment has an effect on crime; I have studied the statistics of criminality and in particular of murder over a long period of time, and I fail to see that the death penalty serves as a deterrent to potential murderers: a murderer in the throes of the crime thinks not of whether he will be punished but of whether he will succeed. The death penalty does have a certain effect on the rest of the population, though, especially the segment inclined to think about such things.

My argument in favor of the death penalty is not that it serves as a deterrent but that it serves as moral expiation. Taking a human life is so horrendous a wrong that expiation can come only from an equally onerous ransom. Of course I make the necessary distinction between murder and other kinds of homicide and accept, with modern criminal psychology, the possibility of extenuating circumstances for every crime. But in certain exceptional cases I cannot deny that capital punishment coincides with the metaphysical recognition of the value of human life. At the same time I hope and believe it will be abolished by universal will as the educational and moral level of the population rises.

*

Should I be asked what I consider the high point of my life I would not say it was being elected president, which meant accepting in equal measure a great honor and a heavy burden; my personal satisfaction, if I may call it thus, lies deeper: it comes from having relinquished nothing as head of state that I believed in and loved as a penniless student, a teacher of youth, a nagging critic, and a political reformer, from having found no need in my position of power for any moral law or relationship to my fellow men, my nation, and the world but those which guided me before. I may therefore state that everything I believed in has been confirmed and validated; I have not had to change one item of my faith in humanity and democracy, in my search for truth, or in my reliance on the supreme moral and religious commandment to "love thy neighbor." Speaking on the basis of the experience I am continually acquiring in my position, I may also state that the same moral and ethical principles which apply to individuals apply to states, nations, and their administrators. But my satisfaction does not so much derive from having remained true to myself through a life of great vicissitudes as from having seen the human and social ideals I professed prove themselves and stand firm through trial after trial. I thus flatter myself that in the struggle for the future of my people and of humanity as a whole I was on the right side. That conviction alone is enough to make a life beautiful and what tends to be called happy.

Notes

Edvard Beneš (1884-1948). Masaryk's right-hand man during the War and the Czechoslovak representative to the Paris Peace Conference in 1919. He was the Foreign Minister of the First Czechoslovak Republic until Masaryk's retirement and then its second and last president.

John Amos Comenius (Jan Amos Komenský, 1592-1670). Philosopher, educator, and last bishop of the Moravian church. He stressed the compatibility of faith and science and the importance of practical knowledge. His belief in teaching in the vernacular led him to write a number of innovative illustrated language textbooks. He also advocated lifelong education.

Josef Dobrovský (1753-1829). Jesuit priest and philologist. He provided the linguistic underpinning for the Czech National Revival movement, recodifying the Czech language and placing it in its Slav context.

George of Poděbrady (d. 1471). A Czech king who called for a federation of European nations to withstand Turkish invasion and establish a permanent world peace.

Karel Havlíček (Karel Havlíček Borovský, 1821-56). Journalist and satirist. He was cured of early pan-Slav tendencies by serving as a tutor to a Russian Slavophile family. In biting articles and poems he advocated a forceful Czech presence within the Austrian Monarchy.

Jan Hus (1369-1415). Religious reformer. A forerunner of Luther, he strongly attacked the abuses of the clergy and was first excommunicated, then burned at the stake. His followers, known as Hussites, fought a long series of wars that early on assumed the character of a national struggle between Czechs and Germans.

Jan Kollár (1793-1852). Pan-Slav poet. He called for Slav cultural unity in a long cycle of sonnets, *Sláva's Daughter* (1824).

Lusatian Sorbs. A Slav people living largely in Saxony.

Karel Hynek Mácha (1810-36). Romantic poet. He is best known for his sensuous and deeply pessimistic lyrical epic *May* (1836).

Manuscripts Controversy. In 1817 and 1818 Václav Hanka, a student of Dobrovský, claimed to have discovered manuscripts containing fragments of Czech epic poetry that dated from the ninth and thirteenth centuries. They were in fact Ossianic forgeries of his own. Though immediately questioned by Dobrovský, they did not lose their reputation as evidence of an ancient and heroic Czech culture until Masaryk's out-and-out exposé in 1886.

Božena Němcová (1820-62). Novelist. She is best known for her depiction of Czech village life in *Granny* (1855).

Jan Neruda (1834-91). Poet, journalist, and short-story writer. He is best known for his *Prague Tales* (1878).

František Palacký (1798-1876). Historian. The foremost historian of the National Revival movement, he is best known for his five-volume *History of the Czech Nation in Bohemia and Moravia* (1836-67).

František Ladislav Rieger (1818-1903). Politician. He founded the newspaper *Národní listy* (National News) in 1861 and was for many years the leader of the Old Czech Party in the Austrian Parliament.

Sokol Movement. Founded in 1862 by Miroslav Tyrš as a gymnastic society, it also supported the Czech cause and had a widespread influence on the population.

Wenceslas (907-29). Early Bohemian king known — and eventually canonized — for his Christian virtues. He was assassinated by his brother and is revered as the patron saint of the Czech Lands.

Works by and about T. G. Masaryk
in English Translation

Works by T. G. Masaryk

Humanistic Ideals, tr. W. Preston Warren (Bucknell, 1971)

Ideals of Humanity and How to Work, tr. W. Preston Warren (Bucknell, 1969)

Lectures at the University of Chicago, ed. D. B. Shillinglaw (Bucknell, 1978)

The Making of a State, tr. Henry Wickham Steed (Stokes, 1927)

Masaryk on Marx, ed. Erazim V. Kohák (Bucknell, 1972)

Meaning of Czech History, tr. Peter Kussi, ed. René Wellek (U. of North Carolina, 1974)

Modern Man and Religion, tr. Ann Bibza and Václav Beneš, rev. H. E. Kennedy (Allen & Unwin, 1938)

The New Europe (Bucknell, 1972)

Slavs Among the Nations (Czech National Alliance in Britain, 1916)

The Spirit of Russia, tr. Eden and Cedar Paul (Vol. 1-2); Robert Bass (Vol 3.) (Vol. 1-2: London: Allen & Unwin, 1919; Vol. 3: Barnes & Noble, 1967)

Suicide and the Meaning of Civilization, tr. William B. Weist and Robert G. Batson (U. of Chicago, 1970)

Works about T. G. Masaryk

Beld, Antonie van den, *Humanity—The Political and Social Philosophy of T. G. Masaryk* (The Hague: Menton, 1975)

Beneš, Edouard, *Funeral Oration* (Orbis, 1937)

Čapek, Karel, *Masaryk on Thought and Life,* tr. M. & R. Weatherall (Allen & Unwin, 1938)

Čapek, Milič and Karel Hrubý, eds. *Masaryk in Perspective* (SVU, 1981)

Epstein, Benjamin, ed. *Masaryk and the Jews* (1941)

Hajek, Hanus, T. G. *Masaryk Revisited* (Eastern European Monographs, 1983)

Hanak, Harry ed., *T. G. Masaryk, Statesman and Cultural Force (Vol. 3)* (Macmillan/St. Martin's, 1990)

Hoyt, Edwin, *Army Without a Country* (Macmillan, 1967)

Kovtun, George J., ed., *The Spirit of T. G. Masaryk* (Macmillan/St. Martin's, 1990)

_____, *Tomáš G. Masaryk – A Selective List of Reading Materials in English* (Library of Congress, 1981)

Lewis, Gavin, *Tomáš Masaryk - President of Czechoslovakia* (World Leaders Past & Present) (Chelsea House, 1989)

Lowrie, Donald A., *Masaryk: Nation-Builder* (Oxford, 1937)

Ludwig, Emil, *Defender of Democracy* (McBride, 1936)

Odložolik, Otakar ed. *Masaryk* (Masaryk Institute, 1952)

Pynsent, Robert B., ed. *T. G. Masaryk, Thinker and Critic (Vol. 2)* (Macmillan/St. Martin's, 1989)

Selver, Paul, *Masaryk* (Michael Joseph, 1940)

Seton-Watson, R. W., *Masaryk in England* (Cambridge, 1943)

Skilling, H. Gordon, *T. G. Masaryk: Against the Current, 1882-1914* (Penn State, 1994)

Street, Cecil J. C., *Masaryk* (Dodd, Mead, 1930)

Szporluk, Roman, *The Political Thought of Masaryk* (Eastern European Manuscripts, 1981)

Warren, W. Preston, *Masaryk's Democracy* (U. of North Carolina, 1941)

Winters, Stanley, ed. *T. G. Masaryk, Thinker and Politican (Vol. 1)* (Macmillan/St. Martin's, 1990)

Woolfolk, Alan and Jonathan Imber, ed., *Constructive Sociological Theory: The Forgotten Legacy of T. G. Masaryk* (Transaction, 1994)

Zeman, Zbynek, *The Masaryks* (1976)

Zenkl, Peter, *Masaryk and the Idea of European and World Federation* (Czech National Council of America, 1955)

Index

Other Books by Karel Čapek

TOWARD THE RADICAL CENTER: A Karel Čapek Reader
Edited by Peter Kussi, foreword by Arthur Miller
Čapek's best plays, stories, and columns take us from the social
contributions of clumsy people to dramatic meditations on mor-tality
and commitment. This volume includes the first complete English
translation of *R.U.R. (Rossum's Universal Robots)*, the play that
introduced the literary robot. $14.95 paper, $23.95 cloth, 416 pp.,
illus.

WAR WITH THE NEWTS. Translated by Ewald Osers
This new translation revitalizes one of the great anti-utopian satires
of the twentieth century. Čapek satirizes science, runaway capital-ism,
fascism, journalism, militarism, even Hollywood. "A bracing parody
of totalitarianism and technological overkill, one of the most amusing
and provocative books in its genre." —*Philadelphia Inquirer*. $11.95
paper, 240 pp.

TALES FROM TWO POCKETS. Translated by Norma Comrada
Čapek's unique approaches to the mysteries of justice and truth are
full of twists and turns, the ordinary and the extraordinary, humor
and humanism. "Čapek's delightfully inventive tales ... stretch the
detective story to its limits and, in the process, tell us much about the
mysteries of human existence." —*New York Times Book Review*
  "One of the Best Books of 1994." —*Publishers Weekly*. $14.95
paper, 365 pp., illus.

THREE NOVELS: Hordubal, Meteor, An Ordinary Life
Translated by M. & R. Weatherall
This trilogy of novels approaches the problem of mutual
understanding through various kinds of storytelling. "Čapek's
masterpiece." —*Chicago Tribune*. $15.95 paper, 480 pp.

CROSS ROADS. Translated by Norma Comrada. Two early volumes of stories, with metaphysical tales and realistic stories. $14 paper, $23 cloth, 256 pp.

Other Czech Literature from Catbird Press

KAREL ČAPEK – LIFE AND WORK by Ivan Klíma, trans. Norma Comrada. A literary biography by the novelist. $23 cloth, 265 pp.

THE POETRY OF JAROSLAV SEIFERT. Translated by Ewald Osers, ed. George Gibian. The largest collection in English from the Czech Nobel Prize winner. $14.95 paper, 255 pp.

Three Novels by Vladimír Páral: **CATAPULT,** tr. William Harkins. $10.95 paper, 240 pp. **THE FOUR SONYAS,** tr. William Harkins, $22.95 cloth, 391 pp. **LOVERS & MURDERERS,** tr. Craig Cravens, $27, 409 pp.

FINGERS POINTING SOMEWHERE ELSE by Daniela Fischerová, tr. Neil Bermel. Contemporary stories. $19.95 cloth, 176 pp.

CITY SISTER SILVER by Jáchym Topol, tr. Alex Zucker. The great Czech novel of the 1990s. $19.95 paper, 512 pp.

LIVING PARALLEL by Alexandr Kliment, tr. Robert Wechsler. A beautiful Czech novel of the late 1970s. $21 cloth, 238 pp.

Catbird Press. 203-230-2391, info@catbirdpress.com,16 Windsor Road, North Haven, CT 06473. **Visit www.catbirdpress.com for more information, including excerpts.**